# Making
# God
# Laugh

# Making God Laugh

## Human Arrogance and Ecological Humility

**Anne Primavesi**

*Making God Laugh*

Published in 2004 by Polebridge Press, P.O. Box 6144, Santa Rosa, California 95406.

ISBN 0-944344-69-0


Library of Congress Cataloging-in-Publication Data

Primavesi, Anne, 1934-
    Making God laugh : human arrogance and ecological humility / Anne Primavesi.
        p. cm.
    Includes bibliographical references and index.
    ISBN 0-944344-69-0
    1. Ecofeminism--Religious aspects--Christianity. 2. Gaia Hypothesis. I. Title.

BT695.5P75 2004
261.8'8--dc22

2004040101

# Contents

# Foreword

Two particular aspects of the continuing expansion of Christian fundamentalism increasingly concern me. One is the theological arrogance that lies behind the fundamentalist claim to speak on behalf of God, for the most we can properly do is speak to or about God. The other is the use of this claim to legitimate various forms of violence – in the name of God. It occurred to me years ago that the effects on theologians who make these claims are exemplified in the remark that "the devil fell through force of gravity: he took himself too seriously." The counterweight I propose to this theological temptation is to take God seriously: to let God be God. That means being aware that at best we make God laugh by our attempts to say something meaningful about the absolute mystery we address as God – and that at the very least we must strive always to make none weep.

Therefore I explore at some length the theological weakness of fundamentalist claims to speak and to act on God's behalf. They too would be laughable if their effects were not so tragic – beginning with excluding other Christians from communion and those of other religions from salvation, and finally excluding all other species from the remit of God's love and concern.

In the opening chapter I draw attention to another persistent feature of Christian fundamentalism that should alert us to its human limitations: the exclusive use of male imagery for God. The inherently presumptive character of this anthropomorphic imbalance cannot be dealt with satisfactorily simply by substituting female images for male ones. Indeed, that would only aggravate the problem (and the reader) by replacing one form of metaphoric hegemony with another. But the question mark raised over this state of affairs will, I hope, exercise its critical force throughout the book and so encourage all of us to deal as courageously, inventively, and appropriately as possible with the problem it exposes.

A positive step toward conceptual inclusiveness, however, can be taken by a consistent use of David Abram's phrase "more-than-human" rather than the conventional "non-human." His usage presupposes that we are human only in contact and in conviviality with the larger community of life on earth. It includes, along with the human, the multiple nonhuman entities that constitute the ecological life-world of our personal and global environment. And so I use "more-than-human" throughout the book.

A number of people have made wholesome contributions to the ongoing theological recycling evident in these chapters. Colin Carr, Jennifer Henderson, Mark Primavesi and members of the Wednesday Group have not only worked over many of the issues raised here but have also kept me up to date with the work of the Jesus Seminar. This book is dedicated to them and to that work. I am also indebted to Lucy Mooney and to religious communities I have met in Ireland at Dowdstown over the years who are now centered around Bru na Cruinne, Drumalis and Pairc an Tobair. They have helped me dig deep into the connections between Gaia theory, justice, and peace – and between all of those and Christianity.

Included in this text are recycled versions of work published but now mostly out of print. Chapters two through four come from *Our God Has No Favorites: A Liberation Theology of the Eucharist,* co-authored with Jennifer Henderson and published in 1989 by Burns & Oates, Tunbridge Wells, England, and Resource Publications, San Jose, California. Chapters six through nine are reworked from chapters in *From Apocalypse to Genesis: Ecology, Feminism and Christianity*, published in 1991 by Burns & Oates in England and Fortress Press, Minneapolis. Polebridge Press, Santa Rosa, California, published "The Christian Gene," an early version of chapter eleven, in *The Fourth R*, Vol 14, No 3, 2001. Chapter twelve, *The Wisdom of Gaia*, first appeared in *The Irish Journal of Feminist Studies*, Vol. 4, Iss. 2, and is reproduced by kind permission of Cork University Press, Crawford Business Park, Crosses Green, Cork, Ireland.

# 1

# Making God Laugh

Yiddish proverb tells us, "If you want to make God laugh, tell Him your plans." But to make God laugh still louder, try telling Him what *His* plans are. Those of us who are Christian theologians have generally concentrated so hard on this task that we have become deaf to the divine laughter our efforts provoke. The deafness is due in no small part to the fact that our attention has been so focused on one plan in particular as to exclude the possibility of others. It is usually known as "redemption through Christ," and is assumed to have been revealed directly to us by God.

### Augustine's hypothesis

While over the centuries differing versions of this plan have been proposed, accepted, and in some cases rejected, the blueprint has remained more or less the same. Augustine established a key feature of it when he hypothesized that the first man, Adam, had sinned, and that therefore God had had to reconstruct His original plan. He did so, claimed Augustine, by bringing death into the world: death as a punishment inflicted not only on Adam, but on every living being. Then God sent His Son down to earth to redeem us from this punishment and from its cause. In the familiar words of a Christmas carol, Jesus was born "that man no more might die." Instead we might, as the original plan supposedly intended, live forever in heaven with God.

This theological framework is built on the assumption that death was introduced into the world because of the action of a human individual who *what ambros!*

thereby changed the structure of the universe itself. It also assumes that death is not "natural" for us: that we do not really belong among the life forms that emerged and evolved through continuous natural interaction between life and death. Thus the purpose of life on earth becomes "earning" eternal life in heaven: a possibility itself "earned" for us by Jesus through his death. The aim of Christian Churches, then, is to get as many people as possible to heaven. But those who do not subscribe to the beliefs or conform to the rules laid down by the Churches are presumed condemned to hell for all eternity.

In *Gaia's Gift* I explored some of the implications of this doctrine of human exceptionalism — a precept that makes us exceptional not only in having brought death into the world, but also in our ability to escape its effects. This presumption of our exceptional status has affected both our view of all other species and our own relationship to the earth, whose existence and fate are seen to be bound up with ours in ways which make it both relevant and irrelevant to us. It is relevant insofar as our temporary existence here gives us the opportunity to earn a better life elsewhere. However, earth's own existence and that of its more-than-human inhabitants is ultimately seen as irrelevant — just as the death that Adam brought on them appears to remain outside the remit of redemption through Jesus.

That irrelevance is presupposed in contemporary fundamentalist versions of the divine plan, in which earth's role in the universe is reduced to being stage and background to the drama of human redemption. This scenario envisages the dramatic action of redemption being played out through a series of conflicts between good and evil. They culminate in Armageddon: the final battle on earth between Christ and the Antichrist, from which Christ and those saved by him emerge victorious. The fate of all earth's other inhabitants is, presumably, of no account to the combatants on either side — nor to God.

The idea of conflict between good and evil as the driving force in Christian redemption, both internally and externally, personally and globally, presented itself naturally to Augustine. He experienced it personally in his own struggles against sexual temptation and communally through the tumultuous events surrounding the disintegration of the Roman Empire. Subsequent to that, through schisms, religious wars, colonization, missionary and economic activity, and European emigration to other continents, this idea of life as a battle between good and evil gained ascendancy over Christian imagination worldwide. From this perspective Jesus' own life, like everything else on earth, is seen solely in terms of our gaining victory over sin and death. Many popular hymns (such as *Onward Christian Soldiers*) learnt in childhood and remembered long after Christian practices have been abandoned, have made this view an accepted part of western culture so that we often see life as a competition in which the winner takes all.

On closer inspection, however, both Augustine's sophisticated hypothesis and subsequent fundamentalist versions of why God's original "plan" had to be amended disclose an even more startling, indeed quite laughable presupposition: that we know exactly what God planned in the first place. A corollary assumption is that our knowledge has, so to speak, kept pace with His, according as He supposedly made necessary adjustments to that original plan. The theological justification for this presupposition is found (if asked for) in the claim that God has made His "hidden purposes" known to us (see, for example, Ephesians 1:9). And furthermore that those purposes are most clearly stated right where the claim to know them is made – in the Bible.

This circular argument about the authority and power of disclosure in the written text of the Bible lies behind every literal, fundamentalist reading of it – usually far enough behind to go unnoticed but close enough to give such readings their claim to authoritative status. Later I shall examine one such reading that is widely accepted today, but the general point I want to make here is that successive interpretations and explanations of the hidden purposes so disclosed are naturally couched in terms that make God's actions humanly and (for the most part) logically acceptable to us. One clear example is that because most biblical interpretations and explanations evolved in patriarchal societies and communities, the male gender of the divine planner and the kind of power He exercises over others is considered so self-evident and divinely established as to need no elaboration or justification.

One result of that has been, as Bernard Shaw pointed out in his 1932 fable *The Adventures of the Black Girl in Her Search for God*, that the God Christian missionaries taught her to seek is one made and remade in the image of a white male father / king / conqueror. But when she sets out on her own search for a God who makes sense to her, she is ready to question what she has been taught. Encountering a Jesus-figure, she asks him what God is. "Our father," he replies. She makes a wry face, thinks for a moment and says, "Why not our mother?" Then he makes a wry face.

*The Color Purple / Celie + Shug*

Most Christians still would. Yet one would think that more than half a century after Shaw's experience of Christianity in Africa, we like the black girl should all question the routine acceptance of male images of God. We have, after all, experienced the emergence of feminist consciousness and, in regard to biblical hermeneutics, the effects of literary deconstructivist theories – including the appearance of that now well-established figure, the "unreliable narrator'. (Though in the biblical context reliable in always being presumed male.) In society generally we have shared the ongoing struggle to introduce and implement legislation against gender discrimination of all kinds and listened to the reactions of those who feel automatically excluded from power, whether spiritual or temporal, by the sole use of male imagery. Yet throughout the English-speaking world, in regard to God, it retains its fundamentalist authority.

This authority derives in part at least from the literary dominance of the King James Version, a seventeenth century translation of the biblical texts whose extraordinary artistic value has, as Shaw says, "given it a magical power over its readers." This power, coupled with the royal authorization of the translation, its cultural status, and its modern reinforcement by the global dominance of the English language, has effectively standardized metaphors for God as almighty father, lord and king. And so it is that the Yiddish God, when addressed in English, is informed of "His" plans.

While this may provoke a wry grin from God and from black or white women, the serious consequence of establishing this religious literary and metaphoric exclusion zone around God is the presupposition that God and His purposes are confined by and within it. This brings me to the crucial point that the laughter provoked by our telling God "His" plans arises primarily from the fact that compared to God – who presumably knows all that needs to be known in order to make and implement them – we know hardly anything. Indeed, that asymmetry defines the relationship between God's knowledge and ours. Yet we appear ready to argue on His behalf for plans we attribute to Him, for their outcomes, and for the reasons why He may have had to modify them. Whether or not we hear it as God's, the real laugh is at ourselves.

On a more somber note, we also appear ready to fight, to kill, and even to die on the basis of our supposed knowledge of those plans. I propose, *terrorists* therefore, a vigilant attentiveness to the asymmetry between divine and human knowledge and an acceptance of the disparity between them as the basic theological constant in our hypotheses about those plans. This would introduce a cautionary principle into any claim to know what God knows, and ultimately deter us from engaging in spiritual or physical battle in God's name. The modesty at the heart of this proposal would help to mitigate the dangerous effects of our immodest claims to divine knowledge.

For the truth is that every time I or any other theologian honestly approaches the subject of God, we are confronted by our limited conceptual and expressive capacities. In fact the longer I study the subject, the deeper appears my ignorance of it and the less ready I am to make absolute claims for the truth of whatever I venture to say on God's behalf. When I can, I speak *about* God and *to* God. But I try not to delude myself into thinking that I can speak *for* God — that is, on God's behalf. Recognizing the absolute difference between these modes of speech encourages a theological modesty that is constantly aware of and consistently attentive to the gap between divine and human knowledge.

*[handwritten marginal note: what about the prophets?]*

### Nicholas of Cusa

Being aware of this theological no-go area is nothing new or unusual. In 1437, when traveling with a delegation from Constantinople to Italy for talks about the reunification of the eastern and western Christian churches, Nicholas of Cusa had what he called a "philosophical Damascus experience." The ensuing burst of spiritual energy, coupled with the eventual failure of those talks, drove Nicholas to intense speculation about the very nature of the theological enterprise itself. One result was a treatise he published in 1440 entitled *De docta ignorantia*, (*Learned* or *Learnéd Ignorance*). The ambiguity allows the title to mean both a knowledgeable exposition of human ignorance and the ignorance inherent in human knowledge. Certainly Nicholas believed that an individual who acquires or possesses such ignorance is wiser than one who does not.

At the individual level "learnéd" refers not only to being erudite or acquiring a great deal of knowledge, but also to the fact that it is precisely through that learning that I come to know how ignorant I am of what still remains to be known. At the theological level, Nicholas linked this kind of ignorance with his reading of Paul's declaration that "The wisdom of this world is foolishness with God" (1 Cor 3:19). Our knowledge of God, he insisted, cannot be the proper measure of God's knowledge.

Nevertheless, there is nothing new about the nature of the claim to know what God knows. Christianity formally categorized it as the sin of presumption. Who, after all, could presume to know the mind of God? The concluding chapters of the book of Job drive home this lesson in theological modesty. Exasperated (one might say) by Job's assumption that he and his affairs are the sole subject of divine concern, God responds by reminding Job of the glorious history of earth and of all the creatures who lived here long before Job was born. Indeed, God makes a special point of reminding Job how ignorant he is of these myriads of beings and their history. It is ignorance, not reason or knowledge, that marks our relationship with them — and with God. "Who is this," God asks, "that darkens counsel by words *without knowledge?*" (Job 38:2) Job's response is exemplary: "Behold, I am of

small account. . . I have uttered what *I did not understand*, things too wonderful for me that *I did not know*" (Job 40:4; 42:3, my italics).

Although the word "presumption" has largely lost these theological
connotations, a modern thesaurus still lists "modesty" and "humility" as
antonyms. To the pious Jew, as to the religiously inclined of any tradition,
there can be no "knowledge of God" without a proper respect for the difference between our knowledge and God's; consequently, modesty is an essential element of any claim to know God and / or God's purposes. We may
thus hope to learn of how "small account" we are rather less painfully than
did Job.

Of course, exemplary biblical stories and personalities are not the only
teachers of modesty. Philosopher Arne Naess has learnt it from paying close
attention to the earthscape around him. As he sees it, modesty is of little
value if it is not a natural consequence of much deeper feelings. More important, it is "a consequence of a way of understanding ourselves as part of
nature in a wide sense of the term. This way is such that the smaller we come
to feel ourselves compared to the mountain, the nearer we come to participating in its greatness. I do not know," he says modestly, "why this is so."

Whatever the subject, the source, or the method, real learning fosters in
us the ability to recognize our ignorance at the same time that it increases
our knowledge. This is not a popular sentiment in a "can-do" culture that
both asserts and insists on our ability to master any subject on earth – and
beyond. As for theology and its subject, God, the call to recognize the paradoxical relationship between wisdom and foolishness or learning and ignorance is hardly a counsel of despair or a refusal to learn. It does not imply
that I am and must remain totally ignorant about God. Nor does it suggest
that historical records of human encounters with the mystery of God have
no value. On the contrary, they deserve to be treated with all due respect.

But that surely precludes using them to cloak or legitimate such igno-
ble ends as the oppression or exclusion of those we disagree with. Rather, it
requires modest acceptance of the fact that since I can never have complete
knowledge about God (or indeed about anything else), what I myself discover together with what I learn from others enables me to appreciate that
fact and proceed accordingly. Because I can neither presume nor claim to
know what God knows, I cannot speak as if I know the mind of God. And
neither can anyone else.

Nicholas called this insight "a gift from the Father of Light above". My
concern here is with what happens after the gift is received. How does my
"learned ignorance" affect my understanding of the world? It challenges me
both to learn and to acknowledge the limits of my knowledge and thereby

to be ready to learn from the work and insights of others. It means that if as a theologian I make any claims to know God's plans, those assertions must necessarily be modest, open to scrutiny, and subject to revision in the light of my further insights or those of others. For what seems wisdom to me may well seem foolish to God – or indeed to others; and new knowledge generated by the social and physical sciences often presents compelling reasons to revise what we say we know about God or God's plans.

For instance, we take for granted our ability to live here on earth, view the heavens, and under certain conditions inspect them in great detail. We have come to see this ability as simply part of the human condition. Science, however, teaches us that although taken for granted to the extent that it generally goes unremarked, this gift is truly remarkable. For like our very existence, that gift depends on a fine balance of two opposed qualities. The first is that the atmosphere and magnetic field surrounding earth are not so opaque as to conceal the light of the stars from us. The second is that they are not so thin as to allow cosmic rays to burn us up. The conditions necessary for human life and knowledge, including our star-gazing, myth-making, and metaphysical musings, are delicately balanced between the two atmospheric extremes of healthy opacity and lethal clarity. That dynamic equilibrium is, and always has been, a primary characteristic of Gaia's benevolence to the community of life on earth – a gift created and sustained over eons of time by evolving interactions between living beings (including us) and their environments.

The evolutionary history of this gift forms the basis of James Lovelock's scientific theory (Gaia) about the formation and singular habitability of Earth and its biosphere. I have reflected on some of the theological implications of this history in *From Apocalypse to Genesis*, in *Sacred Gaia* and most recently in *Gaia's Gift*. From this learning process has emerged one unassailable fact about ourselves and our knowledge: the vision afforded us by our earth-centeredness may transcend our physical limitations, but our earth-bound nature makes any claim to a heaven-centered or God-centered knowledge of earth and its inhabitants truly laughable. Claiming heavenly clarity about God's plans, however, has often had effects that are not laughable, but lethal. Consequently we must examine the Christian basis for this claim in rather more detail.

### Scripture and authority

The first notable feature of this claim is its reliance on the canonicity of certain biblical texts as well as their traditional interpretations. This not only implies, but asserts that in those texts God disclosed His plans for human redemption to certain chosen individuals. Not surprisingly, it turns out that they are the same men who declared those texts to be canonical by invoking the authority given them by those texts.

A prime example of this circular argument and consequent self-validation occurs in the 1964 *Constitution on Divine Revelation* of the Second Vatican Council. It cites the following texts in support of the canonical authority of that Council:

> In His goodness and wisdom, God chose to reveal Himself and to make known *to us* the hidden purpose of His Will (Eph 1:9, my italics).

> In many and various ways God spoke through the prophets and last of all, in these days, has spoken *to us* by His Son (Heb 1:1–2, my italics).

In practice, this has been taken to mean that God has spoken to some (men) among us – in this instance, to those wielding hierarchical authority in the Roman Catholic Church. But through a continuing rise in literacy, translation into vernacular languages, and technological advances in printing, these and similar biblical texts have become accessible to all Christians. Since the Reformation this has meant that other people have established interpretive communities that likewise claim the distinction of having been spoken to *by* God, and consequently the authority to speak *for* God. A favorite text for establishing that authority is Luke 10:16, in which Jesus, having commissioned seventy of his followers to proclaim the arrival of the kingdom of God, is quoted as saying, "He who hears you hears me, and he who rejects you rejects me, and he who rejects me rejects him who sent me."

It is worth looking at the Jesus Seminar's conclusion about this saying. Although the Fellows agreed that these ideas may agree with those of Jesus, they voted not to include this in the database of authentic sayings of Jesus. They sum up its function as "a handy credential as the new (Jesus) movement spread and its bureaucracy began to form." It could well have been a piece of common lore that Jesus quoted in some form, they acknowledge, but more likely it was a convenient formula adapted by the movement's leaders.[1]

This considered judgment is a far cry from the fundamentalist claim of authority to speak on God's behalf, an arrogation that all too often extends to the interpretation of canonical texts, and in due course to commissioning others to do the same. This closed circle of interpretive authority centered on the Bible is almost impregnable to the revision and evolution of thought essential for the health of any branch of human knowledge. Worse yet, by appropriating and wielding this sceptre of divine authority, such groups or individuals seem to render their theological judgments unimpeachable by any human authority. For they claim to speak not only about God or to God, but *for* God.

The historical results of this presumption of divine authority are graphically caricatured in Shaw's fable. At one point, the black girl meets an old fisherman carrying an enormous cathedral on his shoulders:

"Take care: it will break your poor old back" she cries, running to help him.

"Not it," he replies cheerfully. "I am the rock on which this church is built."

"But you are not a rock; and it is too heavy for you."

"No fear," he says, grinning pleasantly at her. "It is made entirely of paper."

But before he disappears from sight several others come along dressed in different costumes and carrying smaller paper churches, and they cry to her,

"Do not believe the fisherman. Do not listen to these other fellows. Mine is the true church."[2]

In the end she has to run into the forest to avoid them; for they begin throwing stones at one another and, as their aim is bad, the stones fly all over the road endangering all who pass there.

Apart from the possibly benign side-effect of eliciting Shaw's sardonic laughter, the history of inter-church stone-throwing – in the form of theological judgments, denial of others" authority, sentences of exclusion, and actual physical violence – has shown it to be a grave danger not only to its immediate targets, but to innocent bystanders and even to the throwers themselves. It is no coincidence, of course, that the throwers carry "paper" churches constructed of bibles and commentaries and creeds as evidence of their claim to truth and their consequent right to condemn and attack those who do not acknowledge their particular claim. It is all very well for President Bush to state that "Islam is not the enemy," but it is noteworthy that in the aftermath of 9/11, well-known Christian fundamentalists who have assailed Islam have assumed not only that Muslim fundamentalists represent the true Islamic faith, but also that like them all Muslims apply fundamentalist interpretive techniques to their sacred scriptures.

One fundamentalist reading of the Christian canon has for centuries wrought untold havoc by presuming to declare on God's behalf whether He has assigned people who have died to heaven or to hell. This disposition is made on the basis of whether in His divine wisdom God has chosen them for redemption or damnation – or in simple terms, whether He has finally judged them good or evil. That judgment is supposedly based on their agreement or disagreement with certain fundamentalist Christian teachings. For example, when a friend of mine became a member of a fundamentalist church, she told me that because I did not agree with its teachings about those who were saved and damned, I would go to hell. Or more precisely, that God would send me there. And this she communicated to me in all earnestness – and without a trace of the concern she would have shown had I been ill!

Simone Weil gave this as the reason why, in spite of her love for Christ, she could never become a member of the Roman Catholic Church. For her "the absolutely insurmountable obstacle" was two little words, *anathema sit* (be you cursed, excommunicated). It was not the words themselves, of course, but the way they have been employed and the abuse of power they represent. They embody a curse that may bring a person either to repentance or to eternal damnation, and thus represent a real threat to one's present life and well-being, or, in former times, to one's eternal life in the next world. In its extreme form an anathema prohibited all social, political, legal and economic contact between the excommunicated person and other Christians; the concomitant shame was another important factor in compelling repentance and conformity with church laws. Among the anathematized have been those condemned as heretics, witches, infidels, or Communists; those who divorced or committed suicide; and especially today, women procuring abortions and those who aid them, as well as those who are living in homosexual partnerships.

While sentences of excommunication are no longer nailed to church doors nor their physical penalties imposed by secular authorities, the use and abuse of this spiritual exclusionary power continues. Awareness of and reaction to the effects of this power, whether the restraints employed are physical, ecclesiastical, social, or communal, forms the substance of chapters two, three and four. They are excerpted from *Our God Has No Favorites*, the biblically based title of which is itself a protest against exclusion from the love and kingdom of God.[3]

### Christians in judgment

My own awareness of and protest against the exercise of Christian exclusionary power has its theological roots in a preoccupation with the need for a "theology after Auschwitz," one that sees as scandalous the legitimation of violence against others in the name of Christianity's God. Its existential roots grew stronger as I became variously involved in the situation of Christians in Northern Ireland and was faced with the living reality of such violence. And its target was not Jews, Communists, homosexuals or gypsies, but other Christians; not concentration camp internees, but residents of the cities and towns of my native land; not "foreigners," but fellow Irish people. As Nicholas of Cusa might have put it, the consistent failure to reconcile Christians *to each other* laid the whole theological enterprise open to question. I came to see that the fundamentalist claim to speak *for* God, when made by opposing Christian groups that categorized each other as "saved" or "damned," made reconciliation impossible. For in either case, the presumed right of ecclesiastical authorities to tell others what future God has planned for them not only goes unquestioned, but consciously or not empowers their followers in the constant confrontations between "paper" churches.

As a counterweight to this, a group of us from different churches met in a reconciliation center in Northern Ireland and struggled to understand the truth of Jesus' parables in the light of contemporary biblical scholarship. We found that *we* had to decide (rather than having our churches decide the matter for us) who, if any of us, we could call sinful or righteous, damned or redeemed. And if so, how then should we behave towards each other? It became clear that we were being told by our churches to welcome only those they deemed righteous and to exclude those they deemed sinners from meals celebrated in the name of Jesus. The fact that both groups would have been equally welcomed at table by him powerfully highlighted the contrast between church practice and his practice.

Unfortunately the former is commonly characterized by a resolute refusal to share a ritual meal in his name with those adjudged unrighteous by the church's ruling body. Such a refusal appears all the more scandalous in view of his inclusion of "sinners" among his table companions – a practice that rendered him scandalous to the religiously righteous of his day. This inversion, subversion, and indeed perversion of Jesus' table has shown church laws that legitimize the exclusion of others from the Eucharist on dubious criteria of sinfulness to be doubly risible. And in Northern Ireland, as we acted out the physical effects of these exclusion clauses by forcibly ejecting from the group some of its most rightfully revered members, we realized how far exclusionary church laws have subverted the unconditional nature of divine love expounded in Jesus' parables and aphorisms, and exemplified in his sharing of food.

This is where the Christian divine comedy has moved inexorably towards human tragedy. Just as Dante happily consigned those he loathed to hell and those he loved to paradise, we found a theological tragedy of redemption being played out by the churches. According to their narrow dispensations, those excluded from heaven for sinfulness or not belonging to the right Christian group (frequently synonymous indictments) are assumed to be condemned by God to hell. And that that, in turn, provides the necessary and sufficient grounds for excluding them from church services. It is another damning example of the effects of fundamentalist circular argument.

But our staging of the parables required us to read from an entirely different script — one in which the roles of the redeemed righteous and the damned sinner were played alternately, indeed sometimes simultaneously, by the same people. And the necessarily deferred climax to the dramatic action gave us no certainty about the ultimate fate of any one of us. What seems an absurdly illogical outcome in the context of a guilt and punishment script may be in full accord with God's wisdom.

Dante's poetic license in assuming the role of divine judge is clearly validated by his literary genius. His divine comedy is a superb imaginative exercise and a telling reflection of his life and times. But one cannot construe as a proper use of human imaginative power the canonical license claimed by Christian authorities to decide who is and who is not worthy to share meals celebrated in the name and memory of Jesus. This is especially true when the practical and often lethal effects of discriminatory power employed by Christian hierarchies are in direct contradiction to Jesus' own teaching and practice.

As Simone Weil saw, that power is today deployed *against* the very people — sinners, pagans, the unclean — among whom he was included by the religious institutions of his time. It has been used not only against other Christians, but in even more absolutist fashion against non-believers, infidels, and Communists; against women, the divorced, the mentally ill, gays, and lesbians. Thus it is emblematic of religious fundamentalists everywhere, in that their self-righteous power is always directed against those they claim are condemned by God. For them, God must surely be *against* those whom these self-proclaimed surrogates condemn, and *for* those who use physical and moral force against others in His name.

This brings me to a particularly virulent and contemporary fundamentalist version of the divine comedy that not only presupposes our *ability* to derive God's plan for the world from the Bible, but also claims divine *authority* to do so. A striking characteristic of this scenario is the use of biblical imagery – usually taken from the Book of Revelation, in which the narrative line of the drama centers on the personal, communal, and even physical battle between good and evil.

In Northern Ireland, Roman Catholics are often cast in this script as "the whore of Babylon." But since September 11, 2001, this drama has played more and more on a world stage and within an actual theatre of war, and increasingly that role is given to Muslims. As I noted earlier, the dramatic climax is billed as Armageddon, a cosmic battle between the forces of good and evil in which the latter power, now represented by every potential terrorist, is to be combated and overcome. The denouement is the inevitable victory that heralds the return of Christ to establish his thousand-year kingdom on earth in a purged Middle East.

Belief in the literal truth of this scenario has been progressively reinforced by 9/11, by the supposed "Clash of Civilizations" and by the double destruction of Iraq (i. e. Babylon) in the two Gulf Wars. Those who claim to know the battle plan and its outcome eagerly prophesy on behalf of the God they believe devised it and whose presence at their side, they say, ensures their victory. And they arm themselves – to use one of their favorite metaphors – with a Bible in one hand and the latest military hardware in the other.

Here the relentless growth of Christian militarism since the time of Constantine has reached its lethal zenith, endorsed by a triumphalist theology of the cross whose adherents use it as a symbol of victory – oblivious to the irony that in Jesus' lifetime it was a brutal instrument of Roman oppression. The visual and verbal links between their apocalyptic version of God's plan of redemption and Christian militarism are clearly discernible in the western media's presentations of war, especially conflicts in the Middle East. Although supposedly non-religious, these reports make clear connections between death and punishment: death is inflicted on the "evil" enemy in the most shocking, graphic, and bloody fashion. Its obviously punitive character and impact reinforce one of the most persistent presuppositions of that putative "divine" plan: that death is not natural for us, but is a justifiable punishment inflicted on "evildoers." And in this grotesque fashion we play out yet another self-assigned role in the divine comedy. We have indeed become bringers of unnatural death into the world.

The connection between death and divine punishment is further reinforced through constant use of the categories "innocent" and "guilty." War reports, political debates and official declarations stress pious regret that punishing the guilty evildoer inevitably entails "collateral damage" to "innocent" victims: civilians, children, non-combatants, and above all, any of those on "our" side killed in combat. Furthermore, opponents are depicted and indeed defined as "guilty," and therefore justly condemned to punishment by death. And just as medieval artists used images of thirst, hunger, torture, and burning flesh in Hell to illustrate diabolical punishment for sin, modern military technology ensures that our enemies will be executed in the most savage fashion imaginable.

 Contemporary Christian militarism is a visible and extreme example of the exercise of spiritual power legitimating physical violence in God's name. It does so by categorizing others as evil, as enemies, as sinners, as unrighteous and unredeemed. Yet it should have no credibility whatever when exercised in the name of the God whom Jesus defined in his categorical command, "Love your enemies." And as the scholars of the Jesus Seminar have pointed out, if we obey this injunction to the best of our ability, they cease to be enemies. We have seen this publicly exemplified in our own time by figures such as Gandhi, Aung San Suu Kyi, Martin Luther King, and Nelson Mandela. Each of us will also have encountered individuals, like some of those I met in Northern Ireland, who live out this paradoxical precept without publicity and in the most extreme circumstances.

### God has no favorites

Let us now return to what I said about human knowledge of God being confined to but not confined by our being earth-centered. The vision of God conveyed in the earth-centered life and teaching of Jesus consistently transcends and subverts the traditional Christian idea of God's plans for the world. Jesus' refusal to exclude others from table fellowship on grounds of their unclean religious status constantly subverts our idea of how God's wisdom might categorize us.

In the final thesis of his 1517 Heidelberg Disputation, Luther offered us a vision of this wisdom that goes well beyond the foolish parameters of conventional Christian teaching. Human love, he says, seeks a beautiful, loveworthy object. It decides, on the basis of human criteria such as beauty, whether or not something or someone is to be loved. Divine love, however, creates the loveworthiness even as it bestows love on its object. In what appears to us an indiscriminate fashion, the love of God flows forth unconditionally: it flows towards those we consider unlovely, those we judge to be sinners, evil persons, fools and weaklings. Therefore sinners are not loved because they are beautiful, but are "beautiful" because they are loved by God. Although human love commonly avoids those we call sinners or evildoers, Jesus sought them out. He said, "I am not come to call the just, but sinners" (Matt 9:13).

For those who call Jesus "Messiah", this aspect of his life is underlined in an Hasidic parable. A young Hasid, a follower of the great Maggid of Mezeritch, married the daughter of a fierce Mitnagged who forced him to choose between his family and his Rebbe. But after a few years he could not resist the impulse to visit the Maggid. When he returned, his angry father-in-law marched him to the local rabbi for judgment. The rabbi consulted the *Shulkhan Arukh* and decreed that since he had broken his promise he had to divorce his wife immediately. The young man found himself on the street without any support. Inconsolable, he sickened and died. When the Messiah comes, the young man files a complaint against his father-in-law and against the rabbi. The former says, "I obeyed the rabbi." The rabbi says, "I obeyed the *Shulkhan Arukh*." And the Messiah says, "The father-in-law is right, the rabbi is right and the Law is right." Then he kisses the young man and says, "But I, what have I to do with them? I have come for those who are not right!"

It is an historical fact that whatever their religious persuasion, the Messiah's official followers have not kept faith with his visionary statements. But this does not detract from their truth. As later chapters will show, they are as startling, paradoxical, transcendent, and subversive now as when they were attributed to Jesus in the canonical gospels. They directly contradict the rationale of the officially proposed "divine" plan for human redemption and its "paper" authority. As we move further and further from the lived experience of the communities who knew Jesus yet still seek to live out his vision within a global community scarred by exclusiveness of all kinds, we increasingly need to renew our sense of their essential – though to us para-doxical – truth. Were we to take these statements as our norm and blue-print, for instance, a radical enhancement of our interreligious relationships would quickly follow.

But that is not, I would say, our primary challenge at present. To take the wisdom of non-exclusiveness seriously today means taking it far beyond its human parameters. For just as the power to exclude other human beings from Church life and practice has been used in a vain attempt to establish for us (and for God!) who was and is "in" or "out" of the closed circle of divine companionship, so Christian theologians have assumed the right to decide for God (and us) what creatures – ever since the beginning of life on earth – have enjoyed a relationship with Him. Only us, we have been told. Or rather, only some of us.

But constructing an exclusion zone around God rests on some truly laughable assumptions. For example, God forcefully points out to Job his mistake in assuming that the relationship between God and the community of life on earth can be confined to the human epoch – perhaps a half million years out of four to five billion. Today we might wish to extend our view further, to the fifteen billion years of our solar system's existence. In either case, the assumption is that no relationship existed between God and the earth community (or any other) in the billions of years before our emergence.

It is also assumed that human relationships with God have not changed during the evolution of our species – from preliterate times to the development of the phonetic alphabet, writing, printing and on to today's era of mass media. This in turn is taken to indicate that interpretations of two-thousand-year-old biblical texts by Christian leaders today can give a precise account of (or more precisely, entirely discount) the prehistoric prehuman relationship between God and all life on earth. But this self-serving claim is likewise roundly denounced *within those same texts*.[4]

The Gospel of Thomas attributes this saying to Jesus:

If your leaders tell you,
Look! The kingdom (of God) is in heaven!
Remember.
The birds who fly the heavens have always known this.
If they say
It is in the seas!
Remember.
The fish have always known it (Thom 3).

The laughter at our presumption sounds increasingly hollow as we reckon with the palpable effects of religious claims to human exceptionalism on our relationships with other sentient beings and with the Earth itself. For we seem most exceptional in our desire and ability to disrupt the equilibrium of complex natural systems that have evolved over billions of years. This is evident not least in our capacity for and obsession with inflicting destruction on these systems and on those lives they support. The legitimation of violence that is an integral part of exclusionary religious power has worked powerfully and consistently to degrade the more-than-human and the natural life relationships within the whole Earth community. It presumes that once humans emerged, the God who made the heavens and the earth relinquished all concern for the earth itself, and for the fate of the more-than-human members of the community inhabiting it. It presupposes that their interests or concerns were never important to God except as they contributed to human well-being and prosperity.

But then, as I point out in chapter six, hierarchical power relationships such as those attributed to God throughout Christian history always presume that some are nearer to the seat of power than others, and that those others are therefore of less value. They are the preordained losers, excluded by their position in life from even the possibility of winning – whatever the prize may be. Today the obvious losers are those Jesus chose as validating our relationship to him – the naked, the sick, the prisoner, the starving, the thirsty. The reward for responding to their need lies, according to the parable in Matthew 25, not in a future "heaven" but in the here and now. And today they may be seen to include those species whose increasingly distressed existence signals major threats to the well-being of all life on earth, including our own – here and now.

The seemingly inexorable move towards tragedy can be halted, I believe, if we make a conscious effort to re-envision our lives in the light of this and other of Jesus' parables, if we acknowledge the paradoxical nature of divine love exemplified in his sharing of food and life with others, and if we accordingly refuse to live as if those *we* call sinners, or evildoers, are seen and treated as such by *God*. In other words, we must learn to acknowledge the difference between divine and human knowledge, between God's capacity for love and ours, and attend humbly and consistently to the distinction between speaking *about* God and claiming to speak *for* God. Only thus do we give God room to be a God whose unconditional love enfolds, and unfolds within, the whole community of life on earth.

### The rich fool

Another parable attributed to Jesus serves to sum up what I have said and lead into what follows. It shows that, as I said earlier, what seems wisdom to us – that is our attitudes to earth's material resources, and the plans we make in regard to them – may well seem foolishness to God. In fact, it is notable for spelling this out.

Luke's gospel contains the canonical version of the parable of the rich fool, and a shorter one appears in the Gospel of Thomas. Together with the appended passage in Luke that contains God's response, both are given a pink rating by the Jesus Seminar, indicating the considerable likelihood that they accurately represent Jesus' words. In both passages the narrative comes to an abrupt, unexpected conclusion. The better known, extended version in Luke reads as follows:

> The land of a rich man brought forth plentifully and he thought to himself, "What shall I do, for I have nowhere to store my crops?" And he said, "I will do this: I will pull down my barns and

build larger ones; and there I will store all my grain and my goods. And I will say to my soul, 'Soul, you have ample goods laid up for many years; take your ease, eat, drink and be merry'." But God said to him, "Fool! This night your soul is required of you and the things you have prepared, whose will they be?" (Luke 12:16b–20).

This parable can be heard in a number of different ways: as a midrash on a passage in Ben Sira (Sir 11:12–28), or as a piece of folk wisdom found in aphoristic form in many cultures. The range of meanings also includes that of the English colloquialism, "You can't take it with you," as well as the sardonic comment of Ernest Bramah's Chinese sage Kai Lung: "He who thinks he is raising a mound may in reality be digging a pit." Today I hear it as an ecological parable intended to shock those of us with ample resources into awareness of what we as a species are doing to those who have none. It is all too easy to envision the mounds of tailings raised as minerals are extracted; the thousands of huge silos filled with wheat, corn and beans; the temperature-controlled pits in which thousands of barrels of wine mature — and all carefully protected from those who cannot afford to buy these or any other goods, or food, or drink.

The barns of the parable can also be seen as exemplifying the folly of short-term policies that take no account of their present or future effects. Some biblical commentators find in this parable an allusion to the biblical idea of "the end time," But it has an even stronger contemporary eschatological twist. For if the fool represents the human species, then our present reckless accumulation of natural resources means that future generations will have none to inherit. So what will *they* live on? God's question can thus be heard another way: "Fool! Will there be anyone to inherit these possessions?" To adopt Kai Lung's vivid imagery, we are so intent on raising the mound before us that we ignore the empty pit left for those coming after us.

As far as I know, this is the only instance in the canonical scriptures where God (in person, so to speak) is said to address someone as "Fool." It is, therefore, as definitive a biblical statement as we are likely to find of the difference between our knowledge and God's and of our wisdom as appearing foolish to God. Especially striking is God's comment on our making plans that appear wise to us, but are supremely foolish in that they ignore the fact that we must die. I note too that although the parable cites God's reference to this obvious fact, it does not say that God punished the rich fool by condemning him to death that same night. There is no need for God to intervene. To read the parable that way is to assume that God uses death in order to punish us for our folly, and is therefore in some measure responsible for the effects of that folly. Not so. God's response does, however, recognize that our actions affect all who come after us, human and more-than-human alike. If our response to the parable were to embody this lesson, then we might be accounted wise – theologically as well as ecologically.

For me, this parable signifies above all else the importance of how and with whom we share – or don't share – food. Indeed Jesus' parabolic behavior and teaching in this regard demonstrates the kind of practical as well as theological wisdom required today. This apparently simple message will recur again and again in many different contexts throughout this book.

# 2

# The Witness of Disciples

This chapter and the following two were written in 1989 as the opening argument in a liberation theology of the Eucharist developed in the light of Jesus' own life and teaching. This involved, as I said in the Introduction, making clear the disparity between that and present day church laws that both rely on and demonstrate the power of inter-Christian exclusionary practice. In Northern Ireland that power is physically displayed in walls built by public authorities in order to separate Protestant from Catholic. These visible barriers are supported materially, psychologically, and religiously by both sides. Co-author Jennifer Henderson and I attempted to breach them, or rather the theology supporting them, focusing our attempt on a close reading of Jesus' use of parables together with a detailed commentary on the context of his exemplary and scandalous sharing of food and drink.

As recorded in the canonical gospels, both his teaching and his way of life disclose – to those who have eyes to see – a Jesus who refuses to separate the "worthy" from the "unworthy." This leaves him free to witness to the all-inclusive love of God. But it does disrupt the conventions of religious separatedness not only within his own faith community but also within those then inimical to his. As it still does.

### At the well in Samaria

The existence of this disruptive force emerges through the close reading of a story about Jesus in the Gospel of John (John 4:5–42). Jesus and his disciples are passing through Samaria on their way to Galilee. Jesus says he is weary and sits down by a well while his disciples, who have been baptiz-ing people, go to buy food. A Samaritan woman comes to the well to draw water and Jesus asks her for a drink. In accordance with the author's inserted observation that Jews have no dealings with Samaritans, the woman expresses astonishment that he asks her for a drink. She knows that Jews consider Samaritan women to be doubly unclean — indeed the term itself was synonymous with uncleanliness.[1]

In the ensuing dialogue Jesus responds to the woman by saying that if she knew whom she was talking to, she would ask him for living water and he would give it to her. She misunderstands: he has no jar and the well is deep; how would he get it? Is he greater than Jacob who gave the well to the Samaritans? Jesus replies that whoever drinks water from this well will thirst again, but those who drink the water that he gives them will never thirst. The woman asks him for this water, "that I may not thirst, nor come here to draw."

The geography of the story places the well about a mile from the city, and the time of this encounter as the sixth hour — noon — the hottest time of day. That means Jesus is there at the very time when the Samaritan women, who must toil under oppressive conditions to keep hunger and thirst at bay, come to draw water. He tells the woman to call her husband and she replies that she hasn't one. Jesus agrees: she has had five, and the present one is not her husband. The woman realizes that he knows a good deal about her life even though he has never seen her before. As Nathaniel had done earlier (John 1:49), she responds to this display of unaccountable knowledge by acknowledging him as a prophet.

The ensuing conversation between them contains some of the most profound statements in the canonical Gospels. The Father is to be wor-shipped in spirit and in truth and without regard to place; for God is spirit and so not tied to place; she seems to have an inkling that Jesus may be the Messiah; and he affirms that he is.

When the disciples return they are astonished to find him talking to a woman. The evangelist underlines their astonishment by noting that none of them felt able to voice their perplexity. C. K. Barrett observes that although this incident has no parallel in the Synoptic Gospels, "Luke's spe-cial interest in Samaritans and women (as in other despised classes) [sic] may be compared."[2] It seems even more to the point here to say that Luke records *Jesus* showing a special interest in Samaritans, women and other despised classes. The important point is that the astonishment of the disci-ples at his conduct was remembered by his contemporaries and recorded for posterity by the authors of Luke and John. And we may assume that the disciples' astonishment and its implicit note of censure was noticed by the woman herself.

She then returns to the city, leaving behind her the water jar from which Jesus has drunk, and says to the people, "Come and see a man who told me all I ever did. Is he not the Messiah?" Here is another echo of Philip's call to Nathaniel (John 1:45).

While in response to her call the Samaritans make their way to him, the disciples urge him to eat. But he refuses, telling them that his real food is to do the will of God. Then the author provides another narrative insert: "Many Samaritans from that city believed in him because of the woman's witness." The Greek word here rendered as "witness" was previously used to describe John the Baptist (John 1:7). Barrett comments, "To bear witness is the task of a disciple. The woman joins with John the Baptist as witness, and in fact precedes the apostles."

The re-discovery of her discipleship (by biblical scholars) does not depend only on her playing the same role as John the Baptist. In his account of Jesus describing the woman's missionary accomplishments to the disciples, the evangelist uses the technical New Testament Greek verb for labor *kopian* (cf. 1 Cor 15:10; 16:16): "I have sent you to reap what you have not labored for. Others have labored and you have come to enjoy the fruits of their labor." The common rejoicing of sower and reaper can be seen to suggest that Jesus is identifying with the woman rather than with the disciples. As he has labored with her, and she with her neighbors, now they are together reaping the harvest of those Samaritans who have come to believe. These, one presumes, would become the foundation of the flourishing Samaritan Church recorded in Acts 8 and 9.

In addition to providing a clear statement of the discipleship of both women and men, this narrative can be read as part of Jesus' kingdom vision. In the kingdom parable of the Last Judgment, Jesus is identified with those who are oppressed here and now (Matt 25:31–46). His relationship with the Samaritan woman makes this identification plain. He introduces himself to her as someone who is thirsty and she gives him something to drink. That is the kernel of the story. Read in conjunction with Matthew 25, it becomes a startling assertion about the nature of the kingdom and a challenging declaration of who can claim to be part of it.

In this instance, the woman responds to Jesus' need, although as a Samaritan who normally scorns and is scorned by Jews, she would be religiously justified in refusing him a drink. She even leaves her water-pot beside him while she returns to the city. Her compassion for him springs from her own experience of thirst and not from any hope of a heavenly reward. She identifies with him in his need; he identifies her with those who are blessed because they respond to present needs: "I was thirsty and you gave me drink."

Matthew 25:31–46 is a parable of judgment that likewise reverses expectations of who is blessed and why: "Lord, when did we see you hungry? . . ." As in Luke's famous parable about a Samaritan (Luke 10:26f.), the despised outsider is the one who lives by the Law and is blessed for it. The Samaritan woman similarly reveals the failure of the official representatives of orthodoxy to recognize the Law's demands personified in those around them. Indeed, the condemned in Matthew 25 protest that they didn't even see Jesus, and the disciples disregard Jesus' need for a drink in their shock at his accepting one from a Samaritan woman.

This disjunction or inversion of values that makes its bite felt in the parables precisely signals their value for a theology that demands a radical change of outlook. In the context of eucharistic hospitality, it calls for a move away from the oppressive security of Church pronouncements about those worthy to share that hospitality. It frees us, indeed compels us to show love towards and to minister to the hunger and thirst of others regardless of their status or orthodoxy. Christ and the "untouchable" woman drank from the same vessel and from the same well.

To the Jews, the Law of Moses was the "Gift of God." Jesus' parabolic behavior towards this Samaritan woman and hers towards him shocks us into seeing that the Law is truly understood only by those who receive and in turn dispense that gift and its transforming power in ways that benefit someone in need. Moreover, he personifies a humility that is prepared to receive God's material gifts from those one has been taught to despise. If a heretic, and a woman at that, can meet Jesus' needs by ministering to him, what does this say to those of his Church who refuse to recognize the ordination of women to the ministry? Neither is there comfort here for fundamentalist Christians who range from neutral to positively antagonistic on the issue of sharing the Eucharist with Catholic Christians – nor for Orthodox Christians who will share it with neither.

This exemplary story resonates with and reaffirms what we know about Jesus' table companionship in his own time. That, and its power to revision our Eucharists now, has been ably summed up by liberation theologian Juan Luis Segundo:

> Not only does Jesus point out that [human] legalistic traditions have been taking the place of God's authentic commandments. He also asserts that even the latter – considered "apart from" the

human being – do not constitute the will of God as a generator of moral values (Mark 7:1–23). God does not come to human beings with pre-established moral recipes. He wants them to establish their morality in accordance with their intentions – freely, from within themselves, and accepting the risk entailed. And to say it once again: only those whose intentions are based on love correctly understand the useful sense of the Commandments.[3]

In the light of all this, one wonders how church representatives can fail to hear the solemn censure contained in Matthew's parable: "I was hungry and you gave me no food, I was thirsty and you gave me no drink" (Matt 25:42). Long familiarity with the Samaritan woman's story has, I think, dulled us to its jolting impact. But once alerted to the outrage that occasioned its being recorded, we might feel a like outrage about Eucharistic practices in our own time.

### Outrage at events at the well

The Gospel narrative alternately reveals and conceals the outrage. At a first reading the woman's own shock is understandable; as is that of the disciples. But these obvious reactions conceal the real scandal to both of them revealed in successive readings. The first and most evident shock is that of the woman herself at being accosted by a Jewish man. She knew of the implacable hostility between Jew and Samaritan, the result of a centuries-old antagonism that had reached a new peak in her lifetime. Josephus records that one Passover between CE 6 and 9 some Samaritans had strewn human bones in the Temple Sanctuary in the middle of the night. The defilement caused by this appalling act of revenge interrupted the Passover Feast and added fresh fuel to the fires of hatred.

It is to her amazement, then, that Jesus asks a favor of her. More amazing still, his knowledge that she has been the mistress of five successive men fails to elicit his condemnation. On the contrary, he does the unthinkable: he drinks from the water jar of a Samaritan adulteress. To the Jews, such a vessel would have been ritually unpurifiable. For even without the stigma of her adultery, a Samaritan woman's perpetual uncleanness contaminated anything she touched.

Jesus' summary abolition of the barriers between Jew and Samaritan, male and female, prophet and sinner, clean and unclean, allows her to question him about the greatest barrier between them – that between Mount Gerizim and Mount Zion. These holy places symbolized the battle between Jews and Samaritans to establish rival claims to possession of God's chosen place. The reigning High Priestly family in Jerusalem was descended from John Hyrcanus, who had destroyed the Samaritan Temple on Gerizim in BCE 129. The time will come, Jesus says to her, when God the Father will not be worshipped by discriminating Samaritans on Mount Gerizim or by discriminating Jews in Jerusalem, but in spirit and in truth – that is, everywhere. There is no one place where God is, for God cannot be contained anywhere or by anyone, either Jew or Samaritan.

The demolition of this final barrier is the most staggering revelation of all for her. But her astonishment is transformed into joy that she has found the Messiah, and this joy sends her back to bear him witness in her own city.

This scene is the subject of a beautiful icon. At the top left hand corner are the disciples returning with food. At the top right the Samaritans emerge from their houses. Both groups are looking down at the bottom centre of the icon where Jesus and the woman are deep in conversation under the canopy of the well.[4] It must be one of the few icons to depict disciples looking down on Jesus during his life. But their attitude rightly places them on the same level as the woman's Samaritan kinsfolk, who hasten to tell her that their conversion no longer depends on her witness.

For they, no less than the woman and his disciples, marveled at the conduct of Jesus the Jew: here he was instructing a woman about the Father and how to worship him! According to Rabbi Eliezer it was "better to burn the Torah than to teach it to women." Professor R. Meyer points out that "neither the Old Testament nor the Mishnah knows the feminine form of the Hebrew adjectives pious, just and holy."[5]

Nevertheless, not one disciple questions him directly, as she had done. Perhaps they feared the implications of how he might answer. Some may have heard John the Baptist witness that "he whom God has sent utters the words of God, for it is not by measure that he gives the Spirit" (John 3:32f.). The Baptist had promised that Jesus would give the Spirit without measure. But to whom? Jesus appears to measure neither the recipient nor the gift against the usual religious criteria. The disciples still expected Jesus to follow at least some of the legalistic traditions of Israel. They simply could not conceive that he had offered this woman living water, for that symbolized the gift of the Spirit (cf. 1 Cor 12:13).

### Outrage at stances today

If any of his modern day disciples reading this account do not recognize the scandalous nature of Jesus' conduct, they have not understood the context properly. And unless we understand the outrage felt then, we fail to be shocked today when some of his disciples still cannot accept that Jesus offers his Spirit as freely to women as to men. Or if they do, they cannot accept what must follow from this.

His conduct not only assumes the value of each individual regardless of gender, it also recognizes the value of each and every Christian in the Church at large. Moreover, it clearly implies the value to God of those who do not call themselves Christian. And this being the case, neither can one justify discrimination against them. So while Jesus' promise of the Spirit without measure should at the very least enable us to accept and share the discipleship of other Christian churches, it also requires us to bear testimony to everyone's value before God, regardless of gender, race or creed.

The call to testify to others' intrinsic value acts as a safeguard against the narrow exclusiveness of an institutional church that sees itself and its ministers as having an exclusive mission to dispense the indiscriminate love of God. Such a notion of church arrogantly confines the Spirit (in every sense) to the ordained ministry. Worse yet, by so limiting the illimitable it contradicts the indiscriminate nature of God's love for all, without exception or distinction.

In Jesus' farewell address to the disciples (John 14:15ff.), this insistence on our common maturity in the Spirit and the demand it makes on us is highlighted by the distinction made by Jesus himself between the disciples' dependence on him while he is alive, and the independence in the Spirit  which he desires for them. The living union in faith of Jesus and his disciples is likened to that of the vine and the branches – the sharing of one nature and one life. Jesus prays for the perfection of this life in them and promises that they will receive it when he departs. They depend on him, the linchpin of their lives, as long as he is with them; but after his departure, the Spirit will be their direct connection with God. The Spirit of God  will animate their entire being, making the truth of Jesus known to them as well as giving them the power to proclaim it and the grace to live by it.

Such a life (ideally) creates a community united in love, a community which everyone might (ideally) recognize as Christian. Jesus gave his life in love not for his friends alone, but also for those who saw themselves as his enemies and behaved accordingly. As his love had no limits, so the community united in it will set no bounds to its love either. This love is not simply an abstract concept: it can be said to have cost Jesus his life. He made no secret of the cost to his disciples either. During his life he was reckoned to be the friend of sinners; on the Cross he was identified with the thirsty, the despised and the disregarded for one last and terrible time. It is our identification with the suffering and despised Christ which reminds us that "martyr" and "witness" are the same word in Greek. Indeed, our identi-fication with Jesus may well include the pain of being publicly identified with the needy, the starving, the outcast, the heretic and the schismatic.

Re-reading the above chapter fifteen years or so after it was written, I am, if anything, even more struck by the truth it seeks to disclose and embar-rassed by my failure to live up to what it demands of me. The encounter between Jesus and the Samaritan woman that subverts both of their legalis-tic religious traditions proclaims its truth more powerfully than ever today in face of the legitimized and continuing separatedness of religious bodies. It challenges us every time we invoke our own historic traditions in order to make exclusive claims to know God's purposes for ourselves or in regard to others. And as those claims are pressed with increasingly lethal effects, so does the need increase to recognize the story's diachronic subversion of reli-gious norms.

I therefore record my respectful dissent from the judgment of the Jesus Seminar when, in *The Five Gospels*, the scholars sum up John's account of the encounter between Jesus and the Samaritan woman as follows: "In this entire passage, John has done no more than collect common wisdom and invent compatible sayings that he has then ascribed to Jesus."[6]

No more than that?

# 3

# The Witness of Jesus

The previous chapter was written after I had had the benefit of reading John Dominic Crossan's powerful exposition of parable in the first (1975) edition of his book *The Dark Interval: Towards a Theology of Story*. Now I find that in this chapter and the next Jennifer Henderson and I anticipated his advice to build up our picture of the historical Jesus from "the most plausibly original materials" – that is, those with multiple or at least plural attestation. In *Jesus: A Revolutionary Biography*, published in 1994, he concludes that this methodological discipline points to the earliest available material. It may not, he says, guarantee truth but at least it "makes dishonesty more difficult." An added bonus, he notes, is that by taking into consideration the discrepancies and differences between the accounts, we see that what those first Christians experienced as

> abiding empowerment of the Spirit gave the transmitters of the Jesus tradition a creative freedom we would never have dared to postulate had such a conclusion not been forced upon us by the evidence.[1]

## The meal at Simon's house

We examined the discrepancies and differences between their accounts and then took them into account when we wrote this chapter. In it we focused on the story of another encounter between Jesus and a woman, this one in the house of Simon the Pharisee. All four Gospels recount the story (Luke 7:36f.; Matt 26:6f.; Mark 14:3f.; John 12:1f.). Close attention to the

29

detail and variation in each account clarifies our vision of Jesus by removing what Segundo calls "all the false pretensions of human beings . . . to grab hold of him, box him in universal categories and thus strip him and his Cross of their bite and scandal."[2]

In Luke's account the woman, described as a sinner, washes Jesus' feet with her tears, then wipes them with her hair and anoints them with myrrh. Jesus does not hinder her from expressing her love and her contrition in this rather embarrassing fashion. As a Pharisee his host predictably reacts to his allowing her such freedom. Simon's argument runs thus: if Jesus were indeed a prophet, he would recognize this woman for what she is, a sinner, and behave according to the Law by keeping a proper distance from her. Further, when Jesus forgives the woman's sins, he is not only breaking the Law but blaspheming, for according to the Law only God can forgive sins.

This illustrates perfectly what Segundo means by "boxing in" Jesus. Having measured Jesus against the "box" of the Law and finding he doesn't fit, Simon is unable to recognize Jesus as a prophet. One is reminded of John 7:49, in which the Pharisees' disbelief in Jesus is contrasted with the belief of "the crowd, who do not know the Law."

In the other three versions of this story, the disciples' response is no better than that of the Pharisee. Their moral objection is based on the monetary value of the ointment that the woman has "wasted" on Jesus. They judge that the money should, according to the Law, have been used to help the poor. Thus they share Simon the Pharisee's inability to accept Jesus as he is, scandalized by his attitude to a sinful woman and his assumption of the power to forgive. Luke puts them together with Simon as "those who were at table with Him."

Matthew heightens the irony by placing the whole scene after Caiaphas and the other leading priests have decided that Jesus must die, and after Judas' decision to betray him. This failure by "one of the twelve" to recognize Jesus as the loving Father's Son is part of their common failure as disciples. John's Gospel also places the story in the context of the Passion narrative, and further highlights the disciples' spiritual blindness by putting their reaction into the mouth of Judas alone.

We can see from the reactions of those at table with Jesus how any law made into an absolute renders even good acts unlawful. Jesus himself calls the woman's action "a beautiful deed." But for the Pharisees and the disciples it is scandalously sinful. Their vision of Jesus is impaired because they circumscribe him and his actions within the letter of the Law. And they do the same when judging the actions of others towards him.

Those at the meal were so boxed in by their own expectations of the Law, of God, and of themselves that they could not recognize Jesus for what he was. Neither could they recognize the true nature of sin nor the true value of their own and others' deeds. How are we to enlarge this tunnel vision? As Crossan suggests, through the gift of the Spirit. Paul states this clearly: "So my brothers, the death of Christ on the Cross has made you dead to the claims of the Law... and we are free to serve God not in the old obedience to the letter of the Law, but in a new way, in the Spirit" (Rom 7:4–6). This recognizes the need for us to move from the oppressive security of the Law to a liberating insecurity in the Spirit; from pre-established moral recipes to intentions based on love.

In the course of the farewell address John has constructed, Jesus distinguishes between dependence on him and the independence in the Spirit that he desires for us (John 14:15). After his death Mary Magdalen was adjured not to cling to him. Through the Spirit handed on at his death, she and the other disciples received their independence from him, and with it the capacity to recognize his witness to the indiscriminate love of God. This maturity in the Spirit was not something given once for all, but was to grow as they realized it in their own lives with every responsible action, every free choice, every decision. In time, they could even make the momentous decision to admit Gentiles into the New Covenant.

The sinful woman did not base her hopes and expectations on the Law. She had learned to expect condemnation from it, ostracism by the righteous and contempt from ordinary hard-working people. As one who lived outside the Law, she was excluded from the Temple and its liturgy, unable to contract an honest marriage, and a source of contamination to those who wished to remain cultically pure. As with the Samaritan woman, her very touch had to be wiped out by purification rites. When she entered the room, the disciples and the Pharisee together would have drawn back in righteous male solidarity against her.[3]

The idea of pollution by association with women has not died out with the Pharisees. It is alive and well in many Christian churches, most obviously in those that still refuse to ordain them. Augustine of Hippo was convinced that "nothing so casts down the manly mind from its height as the fondling of a woman." The Anglican Archbishops' Commission Report of 1936 on the ordination of women stated, "We maintain that the ministration of women will tend to produce a lowering of the spiritual tone of Christian worship." Fifty years later this view, while not so bluntly stated, contributed to Anglican arguments against the ordination of women. When in 1992 it was at last decided to ordain them, this opposition was still strong enough that dissenters were given leave to have dissenting bishops appointed specifically to minister to dissenters.

The derogation of women rests on many ancient and modern taboos, but in Judaism and Christianity it generally reflects an ambivalent attitude towards sex and blood. In Judaism, menstruating women were untouchable for seven days, and after childbirth for forty or even eighty days. The Christian practice of "churching" women after childbirth (or more precisely *re*-churching them back into the congregation) went on in Roman Catholic churches until quite late into the twentieth century – and for all I know, may still persist. These views, which some churches have retained, often underlie their insistence on a celibate or exclusively male clergy. When Peter Damian discussed clerical marriage in the eleventh century he called clergy wives "bitches, sows, screech-owls, she-wolves, blood suckers, harlots and prostitutes." He urged clergy to kill such women. He was quoted by as recent a Pope as Pius XII as an authority on clerical celibacy.

At the present time the Russian Orthodox Church has threatened to leave the World Council of Churches if the demand made by women to participate becomes too powerful. Thus the institutional downgrading of women has become a bargaining chip to be played in the name of "ecumenical" unity. Since the word derives from *oikumene,* meaning "all the inhabited world," it is supremely ironic that women should be excluded from altar and pulpit in the name of this ideal.

It is encouraging to know that many bishops within the Anglican Communion have seen through this sham ecumenism. But now increasingly strident voices are being raised against others similarly castigated for their sexuality: a fearful symmetry characterizes the rejection of homosexual men and that of women among fundamentalist elements in the Churches.

Turning again to Luke's account of the scene in Simon's house, therefore, we need to be fully aware of the socially justified scorn of the Pharisee and the disciples if we are to appreciate the scandal of the woman's action and of Jesus' reaction. We are so used to seeing Jesus' relationship with women and sinners as "all right" that we may not see how completely "all wrong" it would have seemed at the time – and even today appears to some of his followers. Jesus' witness to her and through her of the indiscriminate love of God was, and still is, scandalous.[4] The Pharisee and disciples who recognized her as a sinner expected Jesus to reject her. Yet though fully aware of her sinfulness, he did not reject her. As in the case of his encounter with the Samaritan woman, this amazed the disciples and challenged their conception of Jesus as a law-abiding Jew. The woman apparently had a different vision of him – and behaved accordingly.

Joachim Jeremias interprets her actions: to kiss a person's knee or foot is a sign of the most heartfelt gratitude, such as a man might show to one who had saved his life. Jeremias gives the example of a man accused of murder kissing the feet of the lawyer to whom he owes his acquittal. He goes on to say that since Hebrew, Aramaic, and Syriac have no word for "thank" and "thankfulness," the context determines the word used to imply gratitude. In such a case, surely, it would be "grateful love." Accordingly, he translates Jesus' words about the woman, "God must have forgiven her sins, many as they are, since she displays such grateful love." He concludes that "only the poor can fathom the full meaning of God's goodness."[5]

Matthew places the scene at the beginning of the Passion, immediately after the parable of the Last Judgment, in which the truly righteous are astonished to find that they are inheriting the kingdom because they have done such ordinary things as giving drink to the thirsty and welcoming the stranger. Luke constructs a dialogue in which Jesus expressly charges Simon with failing to offer the proper gestures of welcome, whereas this sinful woman has, by her spontaneous gesture, fulfilled this condition for entry into the kingdom.

Jesus' assessment of the woman's action is clearly not based on the Law, for it would unhesitatingly judge her the sinner and Simon the righteous one. In John 8:15 Jesus explains the difference in criteria: "You judge according to the flesh. I judge no one." She has acted in the hope that Jesus will not reject her under the Law, and also that she, like other sinners, might be accepted as his table companion. In Luke's account, the spirit in which the Pharisee invited Jesus into his house becomes apparent. Simon had not extended the customary courtesies to him due to a guest from a host. He had offered him no water for his feet. Jesus compares his attitude unfavorably with that of the woman: she had washed his feet with her tears and dried them with her hair. Simon offered him no kiss of welcome; she had kissed his feet. Simon had not anointed Jesus' head with oil; she had poured myrrh over his feet. The drama of the scene, emphasized by the dialogue, juxtaposes the sinners (Jesus and the woman) with the righteous (the Pharisee and the disciples).

This reminds us of how Jesus was identified with the heterodox Samaritan woman. Both scenes fill in the background to the phrase: "This man receives sinners and eats with them" (Luke 15:2). Indeed, it was precisely as sinners that he accepted both of them. Like the Samaritan woman who discovered to her amazement that Jesus knew her as the mistress of five successive husbands, the woman who followed him into the Pharisee's house hardly expected him to declare her righteous. But she did recognize in Jesus the gracious, justifying, saving love of God that can transform the least of us into a loveworthy person. As one of the needy, the poor, and the sinful — all "non-persons" in the eyes of the "righteous" — she was open to experience God's loving forgiveness. Blessed are those who recognize the needy and poor in themselves.

In Matthew and Mark Jesus characterizes the woman's deed as an unforgettable act of love – or, as Jeremias characterizes it, grateful love. It provides the future Church with a beautiful example of how to respond to the extravagance of God's love made visible in Jesus.

That the woman recognized this extravagant love in Jesus' acceptance of her was itself a gift of the Spirit, not one bestowed by the Law. Jesus had received this Spirit to preach good news to the poor, and evoked the same Spirit among those who were poor in the eyes of the Law, of the righteous and of themselves. Like the Samaritan woman, the one who anointed Jesus responded to the indiscriminate love with which God had first loved her and witnessed to it by word and deed.

### Eucharistic meals

The ability to recognize and witness to the indiscriminate love of God in Jesus' table companionship with sinners is still the gift of the Spirit. Today as then, the power of the Spirit enlarges the vision of Jesus' disciples. This gift enables us to look at eucharistic practices that discriminate against other Christians in the name of righteousness and to see them for the scandal they have become. Jesus scandalized his contemporaries by eating with sinners. We, "the righteous," are a scandal to him and to each other whenever we exclude "sinners" in his name.

A major block to our seeing this exclusion as a scandal is the notion that the Eucharist is for those we deem worthy or righteous, those whose unity with us and with each other is obvious and admirable. This spiritual astigmatism begins to be corrected when we recognize our common unworthiness, our real sinfulness, our scandalous disunity, and our own hunger as precisely that which brings us to this table. Recognition of the mystery of God's love for us as sinners who hunger for righteousness is the only condition required for admittance to Jesus' table companionship.

This gift of the Spirit requires a response from us comparable to the grateful love shown by the woman in the Pharisee's house. This means opening our hearts to a generous understanding of eucharistic celebration and a grateful awareness of what it must have meant to eat with Jesus. One of Jeremias' major works, *The Eucharistic Words of Jesus*, concentrates on the five Last Supper texts: 1 Cor 11:23–25; Mark 14:22–25; Matt 26:26–29; Luke 22:15–20; and John 6:51–58. And yet he argues that it is a mistake to suppose that the meals of the earliest Church were repetitions of this last meal with Jesus. He underlines the statement thus: "The meals of the early Church were not originally repetitions of the last meal which Jesus celebrated with His disciples, but of the daily fellowship of the disciples with him."[6]

Basing eucharistic practice exclusively on the biblical accounts of Jesus' last meal has had consequences. He is "boxed in" with twelve male apostles as his sole companions. His actions and theirs on that particular occasion are ritualized as the only valid celebration of the New Covenant. All his other meals are telescoped into this last one. This is a real scandal – indeed one that borders on blasphemy; for it presents him as the one who discriminates at his Father's table in favor of a few select men, apparently excluding even his own mother. This slanderous stereotyping prevents people today from recognizing him as he was perceived in his own lifetime. He was one who welcomed such sinners as the intruder in Simon's house, and who in turn was welcomed at table by sinners like Zacchaeus – and as a result was reckoned among them.

Discrimination against non-disciples, women, and homosexuals is not the only unfortunate effect of using accounts of Jesus' last meal as the paradigm of his table companionship. It would hardly occur to anyone taking part in a modern eucharistic service to think of him the way his detractors did – as a glutton and a drinker. Instead of the joy, the bounteousness, the laughter, and the indulgence in the good things of life that such a phrase conjures up, the Eucharist has become a solemn affair on an entirely "sacred" plane, one that proceeds along rigid lines towards a foregone conclusion.

But it is impossible to reconcile such Eucharists even with the accounts of Jesus' last meal from which the pattern is drawn. John concentrates on the washing of the disciples' feet and their preparation for the coming of the Spirit. Luke includes an unedifying squabble between the disciples about which of them shall be the greatest – and this is their response both to what are now reverently referred to as "the words of institution" (reserved to ordained clergy) and to the warning of betrayal.

Eucharistic celebrations have not remained faithful to the spirit of Passover celebrations, either. In the introduction to his Passover service (the Seder), one rabbi observes that despite its Passover origins, the Eucharist has diverged from Jewish celebration. He also remarks that many Jews are discouraged from holding the Passover because "the freedom festival itself has become slavishly imprisoned in rigid form." This view of the Seder as "an untouchable ritual," he says, may be the result of a linkage between the Passover Seder and the Christian rite. "By reversal," he suggests, "this gives Jews the impression that *just as a Catholic communion is a fixed ritual so too must be the Seder*" (my italics).[7]

The fixed ritual nature of eucharistic celebrations reinforces the notion that the Church's service belongs to a dimension beyond time, history, and change; and that power of access to this higher plane is vested solely in clergy who dress differently, presiding over it in robes belonging to a different time and place, thus making it all too easy to forget that the priest travels the same journey as all humankind and shares the same earthly lot with the world. But if we forget that, says Segundo, then we make the mistake of thinking that the history of the world and of the Church, of human effort and of grace and salvation, are different floors in the same building.[8] This false notion of a dichotomy between Church and world is etched a bit more indelibly in our consciousness whenever the clergy dress and behave as though they alone have been given access to the upper room.

The scene in Simon's house shows the same presuppositions in operation: Pharisees and disciples inhabit a different world from sinful women; there is no sharing of ritual welcomes or table. Sins are to be forgiven ritually in another "spiritual" dimension, for which the ceremonies of the Day of Atonement in the Temple are set aside. Yet the woman's conduct was a forcible and unwelcome reminder that it is in our daily lives that we sin and receive forgiveness, and that this necessarily occurs in the same existential dimension as eating, drinking, welcoming strangers, and lavishing resources on those we love.

Writing of the evocation of the Spirit in John's Gospel, George Johnston recalls the story of the Samaritan woman. Who can she be, he asks, but the world in Samaritan dress? And it is to her that Jesus says, "God is spirit, and those who worship must worship in spirit and truth." Johnston's conclusion from that is blunt but compelling: "Given all that, such worship cannot be sectarian, world-denying, individualist and pietistic."[9]

Simon the Pharisee and the disciples make it plain that, left to their own devices, they would have ejected the woman. The righteous make the rules that control who may eat with them. Beside the availability of resources, access to meals is determined by Law and ritual practice, and the latter is presumed to be governed by those with access to God's righteousness. In Luke 11, when another Pharisee invites Jesus to a meal, he expresses astonishment that Jesus did not wash ritually before eating. These rituals are detailed in Mark 7. In both Gospels Jesus gives one of the harshest responses of his ministry, rejecting a tradition which differentiates between the outside of a person and the inside – that is, what is in the heart. "You fools!" he exclaims, "Did not he who made the outside make the inside also?" As with the parable of the rich fool, Jesus contrasts conventional religious foolishness — which discriminates between what we see of a person and that person's intrinsic value — with divine, non-discriminatory wisdom.

Another example that should give us pause is the parable of the Prodigal Son, which ends with the elder brother angrily refusing to go in and eat the fatted calf with his father. It would have meant sitting at the table with a brother who had "devoured" their father's living with harlots. Christian hermeneutics present the elder brother as a jealous, perverse, and benighted man. Yet how do many Christians today react to the prospect of sharing the cup with those they deem social and moral outcasts?

### Righteousness and ritual exclusion

For many years the Roman Catholic Church practiced an internal sanction by encouraging attendance at the sacrament of Penance before receiving Holy Communion. Although this is no longer the tradition for adults, some churches still require children to make their First Confession before receiving their First Communion, thus perpetuating and reinforcing the notion that the righteous do not eat with sinners. This, as we have seen, is an attitude Jesus opposed with his life. Proper use of the sacrament of Penance may foster the correct acceptance of one's sinfulness before God, and of God's extravagant love which creates righteousness from it. But to present Penance as a means of making oneself worthy to receive the Eucharist is to misunderstand both Sacraments. At issue here, of course, is not the sort of case in which someone has been barred from communion because of open scandal, but the insidious presumption that sinlessness is a requirement for eucharistic companionship.

Allied to this is the assumption that worthiness is mediated through a particular baptismal tradition. A continual tightening up of eucharistic practice in the Roman Catholic Church has led to bishops urging their priests to make certain that those who receive holy communion from them have been baptized in that Church. In practice, of course, the priests could be certain of this only if they required all communicants they had not personally baptized to produce baptismal certificates as they queued at the altar. The absurdity of such a directive should not make us any less critical of the thinking on which it is based. Those who sign papers on behalf of paper churches tell us much about the way they perceive the church.

At the heart of such thinking is the assumption that righteousness is mediated only through church ritual; that such righteousness may be identified with one class of person as opposed to another; and that access to this righteousness is vested in the clergy. Because of these assumptions, the table companionship of Jesus has lost its true bite and scandal. The salt has lost its taste.

Following Matthew's account of his own calling, we read that many other tax collectors and sinners joined Jesus and his disciples for a meal. The Pharisees were appalled: tax collectors were traitors, employees of the hated Roman occupation forces, and notorious for their dishonesty and avarice. Small wonder that they were invariably bracketed with sinners by the ethnically pure, Law-abiding Pharisees who prided themselves on their own righteousness. To eat in such company was defilement, rendering a man unfit for Temple worship. Yet despite Jesus' unequivocal choice of self-confessed sinners as his table companions, some religious leaders even today deem themselves worthy to take communion on the grounds of righteousness while employing this same assumption to turn away from the Eucharist the very people Jesus came to call to his table.

This brings us to the heart of the problem. How can we recognize who Jesus truly is in today's world if he is boxed in by the excluding claims of churches which say they represent him? How can Churches recognize him in one another if they use their power of access to deny eucharistic companionship to other Christians on the grounds of the "unworthiness" of traditions other than their own? And what can be done to change practices that deny access to the Eucharist on such grounds? The way forward is to accept the witness of his scandalously indiscriminate identification with sinners in sharing meals with them. The bite and scandal of Jesus' life was its lack of discrimination, and his refusal to discriminate renders yet more scandalous the bar to ecumenism imposed by Christian discrimination today. The self-image and self-expectation of churches that make and interpret canons of righteousness for admission to eucharistic companionship are the submerged rock, the stumbling block (*skandalon* in Greek) on which ecumenical efforts founder. But this rock can be shattered by our grateful awareness of a Jesus who welcomes us insofar as we welcome the hungry and thirsty. New canons need to be developed that are best defined in contrast to the ones currently used.

At one end of the spectrum we have the Pope saying that dissent from the magisterium poses obstacles to the reception of the Sacraments. At the other we have some fundamentalist Protestants who reject Roman Catholics from fellowship because, they say, their Marian devotions put them on a par with Mormons and Muslims. Somewhere in between can be found the kind of attitude reported in a survey by an American Lutheran theological student. He went to a number of Lutheran church services dressed cleanly but informally in a sweat shirt and jeans, and found himself rejected in fact if not by declaration. Few ushers acknowledged his presence at all; when they did, it was only to direct him to the back of the church.

The most consistent contemporary attitude towards inclusion in and exclusion from prayer and table is revealed in the disconcerting experience of a Benedictine monk who traveled in the Christian East as a lay pilgrim and student. In some monasteries he was excluded from prayer and table because he was not a communicant of the Orthodox Church. In one instance this meant being denied entry into the church during services, and taking his meals alone. In another he could attend services, but had to stay in the vestibule between church porch and nave; and he was obliged to eat at his own table just outside the refectory door, carefully separated from monks and Orthodox guests.[10]

The justification for such exclusion was and is based on time-honored distinctions between orthodox, heretic, and schismatic. Its distinctive feature is a consistent attitude towards sharing food. Ordinary meals, blessed bread, and eucharistic host are all seen as valid expressions of companionship. Joachim Jeremias stresses that to the oriental mind symbolic action means more than it does to us. For the oriental, table fellowship is a fellowship of life, and therefore Jesus' acceptance of the outcasts into table fellowship would automatically be understood as both an offer of salvation and the assurance of forgiveness to guilty sinners. This, he says, explains the passionate objections of the Pharisees: "This man receives sinners and eats with them!" (Mark 2:16; Matt 11:19). To those who believed that the pious could have table fellowship only with the righteous, it was clear that by eating with sinners, Jesus was asserting their worth before God.[11] Jeremias' insight into the oriental mentality makes even more scandalous the present-day practices of some Christian monks.

Our western monk was more fortunate in Israel. There, he discovered, the fortress approach to ecumenism has had to be revised radically. In the monastery of St. Macarius he picked up a booklet that included this comment on Christian unity: "It is certain that, should we divest ourselves of our individual "me" and our ecclesial "me" as much on the conscious as on the subconscious level, unity would without question become a reality."

On the individual and ecclesial levels, self-image and self-expectation are barriers to full communion. They prevent us from identifying and recognizing Jesus in the assembly of his disciples today. Is he not, as the Reformed tradition teaches, the Host and the Meal? But is he not also identified with the sinners who hunger and thirst for the food? Yet like them he is in effect excluded from the meal celebrated in his name, kept waiting outside until some sinful man or woman recognizes his need for food and drink.

Segundo is clear about the nature of this hunger, this "mysterious presence" of Jesus. It is not that he suffers the same material want as the least of his brothers and sisters, but that he is present with them in all that is intolerable and inhuman in their situation. Just as they identify with his suffering. The Samaritan woman who trudged through the noonday heat to slake her family's thirst recognized and had compassion on Jesus' thirst. The sinful woman in the Pharisee's house knew what it was to be rejected, and poured forth her compassion for Jesus in what the gospel writer regarded as an anticipation of his ultimate rejection in death.

Led by the Spirit, we too may come to jettison our exclusive self-image and be free to see ourselves and others with the compassion of Kingdom vision. When this happens, there is a radical re-envisioning of the Eucharist. We turn from the altar and find Christ among the congregation, and particularly among those we have previously excluded. We recognize the fellow-suffering of Jesus in them.

Segundo does not consciously equate ecclesiastical refusal to share the Eucharist with the parable of the last judgment. But he does emphasize the suffering inflicted on those excluded from sharing food with us, whether in church or at table. God, he says, is truly recognized (for who God is and for what God wants) when the individual is freed from his or her misery: "Moreover, if this is not done, no matter how religious one is (see Jas 2:14–17; 1 John 4:20), that 'mysterious presence' will be replaced by eternal absence: 'Out of my sight, you condemned, into that everlasting fire. . . . I was hungry and you gave me no food'. . . ."[12]

Those who debate about Real Presence in the Eucharist should instead be concerned with this eternal absence.

# 4

# The Witness of the Body

*"Eh lass, we're nowt special. We're just put*
*on earth to make the numbers up!"*

This piece of Yorkshire wisdom passed on from mother to daughter captures the view many church members have of themselves. It also tallies with Jesus' description of those who come to his table.

### The great banquet

At another meal in a Pharisee's house Jesus offers his host advice on what sort of guests to invite to dinner, and then tells the group a story on that subject (Luke 14:12–24). In the parable of the Great Banquet, both the invited guests and the host abandon the norms of social behavior. Angered when all his guests send excuses just about the time they should be arriving, the host sends his servant to bring in anyone who can be found. If he cannot eat with friends, he will eat with strangers. The numbers at his table must be made up.

How are they made up? The instructions to the servant repeat the advice given earlier: invite the poor, the blind, the lame, the maimed — and when there is still room, round up those in the highways and byways.

The scenario is so bizarre that while we muse on its improbabilities we are liable to forget its setting. To be sure, Jesus is addressing "the Pharisees watching him," who would recoil in horror from being identified with either host or guest in the story, but more specifically the parable is a response to another guest. This man had taken up Jesus' statement about rewards in the next life for feeding the poor, maimed, lame and blind. "Blessed is he who

shall eat bread in the kingdom of heaven," exclaims this pious guest. This is
the kind of pragmatic morality he can understand. The good deed that is
not repaid now will merit a luncheon voucher in the kingdom of God.

"But Jesus said to him . . ."

As so often, these words begin a saying of Jesus that will run completely
contrary to the hearers' expectations. Jesus' vision of the kingdom in the
Great Banquet parable does not deny the practical morality of the pious
Pharisee, but puts it in perspective. Pharisaic morality, and indeed ours, is
set in contradistinction to the fundamental morality of the kingdom. In
practice people have to make distinctions and choices; for instance, we look
forward to a return invitation from those who have visited us. But God does
not limit invitations. God's gift of life is for every creature; God's love and
morality are all-inclusive. Jesus underlines this distinction between God's
hospitality and ours.

Such parables bring us up short before the boundless nature of God's
love. The feeling of vertigo one might experience on the rim of a bottomless
crater resembles the kind of shock which can be the immediate effect of
parable. The head spins at the prospect of a love that will not discriminate.

A Jewish parable along these lines induces the same vertigo:

> God showed Moses the great treasure troves in which are stored up
> the various rewards for the pious and the just, explaining each sep-
> arate one to him in detail: in this one were the rewards of those
> who give alms; in that one, of those who bring up orphans. In this
> way He showed him the destination of each one of the treasures,
> until at length they came to one of gigantic size. "For whom is this
> treasure?" asked Moses, and God answered: "Out of the treasures
> that I have shown thee I give rewards to those who have deserved
> them by their deeds; but out of this treasure do I give to those who
> are not deserving, for I am gracious to those also who may lay no
> claim to My graciousness, and I am bountiful to those also who
> are not deserving of My bounty."[1]

Jesus makes the same point in the parable of the Great Banquet. Those
who taste the banquet do so because the host insists. The house is to be
filled. This takes priority over everything else. There are no criteria for the
guests: they can neither refuse nor repay hospitality. The poor, maimed,
blind and lame are "brought in." Those in the highways and hedges are
"compelled." These are the very categories of people forbidden entry into
the sanctuary to offer bread to God (Lev 21:18ff.).

Nor does the invitation discriminate between those who belong to the city (the insiders, the Jews), and those beyond its gates (the outsiders, the Gentiles), except that the last mentioned – transients and the homeless – are to be forced to come in and make up the numbers. And no distinctions are to be made among velvet, white, and blue collars; indeed, some have no collars at all.

The shock of this parable, like the impact of a rock thrown into a pool, shatters first the surface calm of the community around Jesus, but its waves still ripple out to disturb us today: they bring home to us the scandal embodied in the examples of Church discrimination mentioned in the preceding chapter. Those turned away from our communion tables by contemporary Church canons of worthiness are the modern counterparts of the guests brought in to the Great Banquet: they have no insider right of access, no properly completed baptismal certificates – perhaps not the right collars. And what welcome is there for those with bills of divorce in their pockets?

Yet those very churches that discipline the divorced as unworthy communicants have been known to demand divorce to establish worthiness. Writing of the mainline mission-founded churches in Africa, Kofi Asare Opoku says that they assume that one cannot sincerely love Christ and be a polygamist at the same time. Therefore they bar polygamists from the Lord's Supper unless the man divorces all his wives except the first. And although the sufferings that many people have gone through before being judged "righteous" enough to partake of the Lord's supper defy description,

> "the church considers this of little consequence, since in its view divorcing all one's wives and imposing untold hardship on many women and children is what Christ demands of those who love him."[2]

This distortion of Christ's demands has arisen, says Opoku, because the church uses the Lord's Supper as an instrument of discipline. Yet Jesus' own table companionship was condemned by the religious authorities of his day because he ignored their discipline when he ate and drank with tax-collectors and sinners.

Then what is the biblical authority, Opoku asks, for this exclusion which separates the "righteous" (monogamists) from the "unrighteous" (polygamists)? Does a person who has more than one wife necessarily cease to believe in Jesus as his Savior? How can the church assert that such a person cannot believe in Jesus Christ?[3]

The shock we experience today when juxtaposing exclusionary church disciplines with the inclusive invitation of the Great Banquet parable forces us to recognize the failure of the churches to witness to the indiscriminate love of God. This is especially scandalous when, gathered publicly as Christ's body, we give thanks for that very love which our exclusions betray.

But perhaps the deepest shock is felt when we face the mystery of our own invitation. Since we can make no claim on God's graciousness, have we no right to God's bounty? Must we be reckoned with the riff-raff, with those who have to be dragged in? Do we even want to be there if the host won't distinguish between the good and the bad, the just and the unjust — if he distributes invitations as indiscriminately as sunshine and rain? Do we really believe Paul when he says, "God has no favorites?" (Rom 2:11)

We are shocked by the contrast between our pragmatic morality and the fundamental morality of the kingdom. But the kingdom vision must be kept before us lest we too easily accommodate it to our own. One criterion we can establish from this parable is our readiness to identify with the "riff-raff" of other denominations. Unless we accept that we are all "nowt special" together, we risk our own invitation to table.

The fact that humanly speaking this is impossible, that our goal is beyond our reach, is both a remedy against downheartedness when we fail to live up to it and a spur to further effort. As Segundo points out,

> No matter how many signs of its power may be firmly planted in history, there will always be a verifiable distance between embodiments of the kingdom and the kingdom itself. The laws of the easy way in an already created world will always be at work against the kingdom. . . . Thus the task of constructing the kingdom with God, of taking the next step forward, will continue in all its radicalness from one generation to the next, challenging every individual and generation to display the full creativity of their love.[4]

Part of that task for us is to keep faith with the kingdom vision of inclusiveness at Jesus' table. This keeping faith is a gift of the Spirit which comes through prayerful reflection on Jesus' parables and actions. On the one hand the parables tell us that we are there to make up the numbers because our host so wills; on his initiative alone, we are at his table. On the other hand, the host in the parable contained in Luke 14:7–10 practices positive discrimination by choosing to exalt those who have humbled themselves. We hope he has already chosen us, but can we accept the teaching that as the "chosen," *we* are among the poor, blind, and maimed? What sort of elite is that?

Acceptance of this is particularly hard for those of us who are not materially poor. Our self-image seems to need to exclude need. Part of the problem of developing a liberation theology in the First World is its emphasis on improving the lot of the economically oppressed. A eucharistic liberation theology does not ignore economic deprivation, but redefines the concept of need within a eucharistic context. At God's table, those in velvet collars are just as needy as those without shirts. The vital link between hunger, bread, and life draws us all together to eat, but this universal dynamic is hidden from the materially rich as well as the materially poor by church practices that legislate for the eucharistic deprivation of some Christians in favor of others. Ecclesiastical classifications of some as needy / worthy means the deprivation of others classed as needy / unworthy. Yet being needy is the only criterion that the God of Jesus applies.

Those approved and those deprived find this uncritical approval equally hard to accept, but if as well as listening to the parables we look at Jesus' own practice, it *must* be accepted. He demanded no poverty standard or means test for those who wanted to eat with him. He refused to make any tests. More than that, he went looking for those who, because they expected to be failed automatically, would never have presented themselves in the first place. To the Jews of Jesus' day, the rich Zacchaeus was as untouchable because of his occupation as the poor Lazarus of the parable because of his sores, and as ineligible a host as a diseased beggar would be a guest. Sin was as contagious as disease.

### Contagion, fellowship, worthiness

This idea of contagion is alien to our modern culture, where public and religious conventions no longer control one another. Christians work alongside those of other faiths or no faith at all without fear of contamination. We invite whom we wish to our homes without preliminary screening. An "open and notorious evil-liver" may offend, but no one imagines his disrepute will rub off onto others by physical contact, less still from a chair on which he has sat.

For the Jews, however, table, house and Temple were centers of purity from which the impure and polluted must be excluded. If this was done, the food consumed in both the home and the sanctuary brought a blessing. It brought life. But if pollution entered the house or sanctuary — as it could from touching someone or something impure — then contagion spread through the family or priesthood, and both family meal and sacrifice brought a curse — and perhaps death. In 1 Corinthians 10:21, for example, Paul distinguishes between the cup of blessing (the cup of the Lord) and the cup of demons. The Jewish ritual system was founded on the distinction between pure and polluted, blessing and curse. It entailed ceaseless vigilance to preserve the purity of the table, the house and the Temple. Being kosher was (and still is) considered a matter of life and death.

*Purity code*

A similar attitude to pollution operates today at many levels outside Judaism. We accept that touch (contagion) is a medium of transfer for good or ill. Hygiene – personal, public and culinary – is known to be a crucial defense against disease. Isolation wards and quarantine are necessary measures against contagion. And even in an enlightened age, various taboos still operate: the common inhibition against using another's toothbrush has assumed nightmare significance in a world threatened by AIDS.

This principle of contagion works at other levels too. "Is there any man here who is fearful and faint of heart? Let him go home lest he make his fellows lose heart also" (Deut 20:8). Optimism and pessimism, heroism and panic are also "catching." And it now appears that ordinary physical and social contacts are not the only ones that affect us, for a number of new fields of study dealing with the connections between mind and matter have broadened our understanding of contiguity. This has emerged from the dramatic shift of basic concepts that has occurred in modern physics. For example, the nuclear physicist Fritjof Capra presents us with a new vision of reality based on "awareness of the essential interrelatedness and interdependence of all phenomena – physical, biological, psychological, social and cultural."[5]

Though not expressed in these modern categories, the Jewish vision of reality that Jesus shared with his contemporaries showed a similar awareness. Like Capra's, it had the positive aim of enhancing understanding of our common interdependence. But it differed in its view of how and why that interrelatedness and interdependence operated. The primary relation and dependence it presupposed was between Yahweh and creation. Yahweh opens the heavens and the womb, makes the earth and the female fruitful. But even in this most intimate and life-giving relationship, Yahweh is clearly separate. In the Jewish Scriptures, the word for holy derives from the Hebrew word meaning "to separate."

The essential difference between heaven and earth sums up for the Jew both the relation and the separation. Like heaven and earth, the pure and the impure must be kept separate, the pure being the proper space for fruitfulness, life, growth, and blessing; the impure or polluted being the space of barrenness, death, destruction and curse. The necessary separation and intimate union between heaven and earth was the basis for the dietary and purity laws. "Be holy, for I your God am holy" was a call to separate oneself from pollution. "I call heaven and earth to witness against you this day, that I have set before you life and death, blessing and curse; therefore choose life, that you and your descendants may live" (Deut 30:19).

This profound understanding of the relationship between Yahweh and Israel, heaven and earth, has been handed on to us by Paul:

> Do not unite yourselves with unbelievers; they are no fit mates for
> you. What has righteousness to do with wickedness? Can light con-
> sort with darkness? Can Christ agree with Belial, or a believer join
> hands with an unbeliever? Can there be a compact between the
> temple of God or the idols of the heathen? And the temple of the
> living God is what we are. God's own words are: "I will live and
> move about among them; I will be their God, and they shall be
> my people." And therefore, "come away and leave them, separate
> yourselves, says the Lord; do not touch what is unclean. Then I
> will accept you, says the Lord, the Ruler of all being; I will be a
> father to you, and you shall be my sons and daughters." Such are
> the promises that have been made to us, dear friends. Let us there-
> fore cleanse ourselves from all that can defile flesh or spirit, and in
> the fear of God complete our consecration (2 Cor 6:14–7:1).

The relationship between Yahweh and Israel was the basis for "cleans-
ing ourselves from all that can defile." The orthodox Jew did not measure
his cleanliness in relation to other Jews but in relation to Yahweh. This fundamental logic must be kept in mind if we are not to fall into the trap of
thinking Judaism merely obsessive about cleanliness for its own sake. In his
study *Paul and Palestinian Judaism*, E. P. Sanders stresses how easy it is to
miss this Jewish logic. Thus when Paul says: "The body is not meant for
immorality, but for the Lord, and the Lord for the body," he is arguing that
one participatory union can destroy another. Even when they are not on
the same level, a person cannot participate in two mutually exclusive
unions.

The stereotypical mother-in-law illustrates the dynamics of this principle. A young couple marry and begin a relationship that subtly moulds
them into a new pattern of tastes, behaviors, and values. The mother of one
of them resents these changes, seeing them as threatening the bond with
her child. If she defends that bond with enough determination, her child
must either sever the parental relationship or allow the marriage union to
be destroyed.

As Sanders incisively explains, we so readily agree with Paul's condemnation of sexual immorality that it is easy to miss the rationale behind it —
a logic that while natural to Paul is foreign to us.

> We might expect an argument that a Christian should not behave
> in such and such a way, since immorality is not appropriate to
> being Christian, since it is forbidden in the Bible or since such a
> transgression will result in punishment from God; but to say that

one should not fornicate because fornication produces a union which excludes one from a union which is salvific is to employ a rationale which today is not readily understood.[6]

Yet unless we try to understand the Jewish basis of keeping table fellowship "pure," we fail to grasp the scandal of Jesus eating and drinking with the riff-raff of his day. We miss the logic of Paul's assertion that "for our sake he made him to be sin who knew no sin, so that in him we might become the righteousness of God" (2 Cor 5:21). We misunderstand the horror behind such questions as "Why does your master eat with sinners?" and the certainty with which he was labeled as one in consequence: "We *know* that this man is a sinner" (my italics). As Jesus placed his body in close proximity to "polluted" bodies, he became polluted. As he shared table and house with sinners, he became one. He ate the same food as sinners, dipped his hand into the bowl of the tax-collector, received the unclean touch of a menstruating woman, and lifted the dead body of Jairus' daughter. This is what Paul means when he says Jesus was "made sin." He participated in the bodiliness of sin, so that we might participate in his body and drink of his Spirit.

Three things stand out here. First, the notion – shocking and quite unbelievable to any Jew – that God has become flesh, has taken a body. Heaven and earth are no longer separate. He came unto his own, and they did not receive him. But how could they? Christians too cannot be complacent about their own ability to recognize and accept the presence of Christ. For many of them it is confined to safe rituals or physically boxed in tabernacles. Finding his presence to be real among those excluded by churches can be just as shocking today to Christians as the physical presence of Jesus among those excluded from the Temple was to the Jews. Their acceptance of the scandalous absence from churches of those deemed ritually unworthy to receive communion raises a profound question over their belief in his "real" presence being confined to bread shared by a cultically pure clergy with cultically worthy communicants.

Second, our efforts to maintain ritual purity have lost the sound basic premise of Judaism that measures human purity not in relation to others but in relation to God. The Jews had as their ideal the holiness of God, and this required them to separate themselves from the unholy. But laws against intercommunion in Christian churches are based not on the unworthiness of all Christians, but the unworthiness of some compared to others. This is an absolute contradiction of Jesus' refusal to discriminate; it flatly repudiates his declaration that he came to seek and to save the lost. If we live with this contradiction and make it church policy, we lose sight of the basic premise of Christianity: he alone knew no sin, yet he did not separate himself from sinners. In relation to him, we are all unworthy and all welcome.

The third point, which follows from this, is that it becomes possible to understand how Dominic Crossan can call Jesus "the Parable of God."[7] He leads us to the edge of the abyss of God's love, where we discover that he is that edge. In his life and actions, summed up in his table companionship, he refused to separate himself from us. He is the one who unites pragmatic and divine morality. For us no less than for the Jews of his day, he reverses all expectations about God. The unique, scandalous connection between the kingdom, the meal and the sinner is visible in what he did and said. The Word of life and the Word of God are completely integrated in him.

Another equally shocking Word is also integrated for us in the Eucharist: the Word of the Cross. Paul describes this too as a scandal, the final reversal of expectation for the disciples. When we break bread in his name, we remember his body broken for us on the Cross and in the bread. This was not only for properly baptized Christians but for all: he made no distinctions among those with whom he ate or those for whom he died. Paul specifically refers to the Cross when he distinguishes between human wisdom and the divine wisdom that we see as foolishness.

An irony of church history has been the making of the crucifix into a barrier called the rood screen. Placed between sanctuary and people, priest and congregation, it separates them as surely as the priest in the Temple was separated from all others. The encouraging vision of the author of the Letter to the Hebrews is lost. For him, the Cross is not a barrier but the point of access, the edge of the abyss:

> Therefore, brethren, since we have confidence to enter the sanctuary by the blood of Jesus, by the new and living way which he opened for us through the curtain, that is, through his flesh, and since we have a great priest over the house of God, let us draw near with a true heart in full assurance of faith, with our hearts sprinkled clean from an evil conscience and our bodies washed with pure water (Heb 10:19f.).

This encouragement and confidence is as necessary for us as it was for those invited to table by Jesus. Zacchaeus lets us glimpse the sheer incredulity with which sinners no less than Pharisees heard and accepted Jesus' invitation. For both, to eat with him meant publicly flouting the prevailing religious conventions.

### Who do we welcome?

What does this demand of Christian congregations? Simply this: that we too find courage and confidence to enter one another's sanctuaries, undeterred by barriers of false righteousness. That we be united in the new and living way Jesus opened for us by the manner in which he shared our common flesh, our bodiliness. Then we can accept truthfully and joyously our common unworthiness, and refuse categorically to test one another's right to share table companionship in his name.

George Herbert expressed this truth magnificently in his poem, Love:

Love bade me welcome; yet my soul drew back,
    Guilty of dust and sin.
But quick-eyed Love, observing me grow slack
    From my first entrance in,
Drew nearer to me, sweetly questioning,
    "If I lacked anything."

"A guest," I answered, "worthy to be here."
    Love said, "You shall be he."
"I, the unkind, ungrateful? Ah, my dear,
    I cannot look on Thee."
Love took my hand, and smiling, did reply,
    "Who made the eyes but I?"

"Truth, Lord, but I have marred them: let my shame
    Go where it doth deserve."
"And know you not," says Love, "who bore the blame?"
    "My dear, then I will serve."
"You must sit down," says Love, "and taste my meat."
    So I did sit and eat.[8]

Herbert concentrates on the presence of God revealed in the indiscriminate love of the host and in the meal itself. We have been discovering that same presence among the sinners made welcome by the host. Thus emerge three characteristics of the mystery of God's presence: as host, as meal, as guest; complete in each, with no one devaluing the others. The first two are common topics in eucharistic discussion, but not the third. As in previous chapters, this understanding of Eucharist also identifies Jesus with those who hunger and thirst now, both those in our congregations and the starving people of the world.

This liberating vision is not new, but rather a re-presentation of the vision of Jesus outlined in the parables and that of Paul in his teaching on the celebration of the Lord's Supper. The first eucharistic assemblies we read of are those he addressed. Jeremias dates Paul's letters to the Corinthians about 54 CE. In their celebrations of the Eucharist, the primitive church at Corinth experienced in a unique way the proximity, presence, and society of its Lord. For Paul, the body of Christ we receive in the bread directly represented the body of Christ in which we are bound together. We receive the body of Christ, and by receiving it we both become and show ourselves to be the body of Christ.

Paul does not speak of eating the body and drinking the blood of Christ. Indeed, his formula does not express the simple equation, cup = blood. Nor does he say in 1 Corinthians 10:1ff. that Christ is the miraculous drink that was given to Israel; but rather that he is the rock from which the water springs. Christ does not change himself into a sacramental substance but is the giver of the spiritual drink and spiritual food. Further, 1 Corinthians 10:16 speaks about the breaking of the bread and the blessing of the cup as sacramental acts, not about eating and drinking.

The conclusion to be drawn from Paul's eucharistic texts is that the body of Christ received in the sacrament forms the mystical body of Christ that is the congregation. If one member suffers, all suffer together; if one member is honored, all rejoice together. . . You are the body of Christ and individually members of it (1 Cor 12:26–27).

Discerning the body today means understanding that the body of Christ given for us and received in the sacrament unites us in the "body" of the whole earth community and makes us responsible for one another in love.

And so the vision of the common person, the woman or man who considers herself or himself "nothing special," can be the catalyst for change in the churches' perception of communion and community. Liberation theology is solidly founded on this. The powerless discover the power to change themselves, others, and institutions when they discover through the free gift of the Spirit that they are, in truth, the body of Christ within the whole earth community.

Herbert describes this discovery and its consequences at the end of his poem *The Invitation*:

> Lord, I have invited all,
>     And I shall
> Still invite, still call to Thee:
> For it seems but just and right
>     In my sight,
> Where is all, there all should be.[9]

# 5

# Thinking Outside the Box

The previous chapter opened with Jesus' parabolic story of a banquet at which the conduct of host and guests runs directly contrary to expectations. It closed with poet George Herbert's equally unconventional account of the welcome to the banquet of life offered all of us by divine love — which differs from human love in its capacity to cherish all of us indiscriminately. It therefore welcomes all to the table, even those who would exclude themselves on the grounds of not being worthy to be there. The poet sums up this vision of all-inclusive love in the memorable phrase: "Where is all, there all should be." For him, to follow Jesus' example means that exclusionary clauses, self-inflicted or otherwise, contradict the very intention that lies behind the gift of divine love to all.

Such stories and poems about banquets often focus on a particular religious insight open to a range of interpretations. A rabbinic version tells of ten men assembled for a banquet. One brings a large fish, another a small fish; one salted fish and another unsalted; one brings boiled cabbage and beets, another brings eggs; one brings cheese, another brings meat from an ox; one brings meat from a ram, and another meat from a fowl. Each takes his share of the ten kinds of food and returns home.

So too, say the rabbis, when a man goes to the synagogue or house of study, he may learn from each of the nine men already there a single verse of Torah, a single interpretation, a single Halakah. Thus each takes away with him ten Halakot, ten verses of Torah and ten interpretations.

Mary Chilton Callaway quotes this story to illustrate the rabbinic view that a single text may generate an infinite progression of interpretations.

Torah is not a puzzle to be solved but a catalyst for creating meanings, and can be likened to a banquet after which the diners return home well fed. Yet the Torah remains unconsumed, ready for the next party who will feed on it.

Nonetheless, she says, the Torah is not unaffected by its readers, because no generation can read it as though it had never been read before. Christians, she points out, instinctively read Genesis 3 as the first chapter in the history of salvation even though this reading is implicit neither in the text nor in the intention of the ancient authors or their translators. Rather, it is an interpretation that has been transmitted along with the text.[1]

### The making of the box

Up to and including the present time, "salvation history" has provided the interpretive context within which Christians read the Bible. It functions much as would a box made to contain a set of books. It fits and shapes their outline, establishes the positioning of each relative to the others, and thus encloses them within a structure of meaning disclosed anew on every reading. In addition, it comes stamped with the hallmark of authenticity by virtue of its having been made, supplied and handed on by previous generations as a precious inheritance given them by God.

It was first made, as Chilton Callaway's example shows, by merging the biblical history of the Jewish people with that of Christianity. One example of this blending – and perhaps the most decisive – was the characterization of the Hebrew Bible as the "Old" Testament, and the early records and reflections concerning Jesus' life and teachings as the "New" Testament. This co-ordination (in the double sense of ordering and ordaining) and these titles rely on and imply theological concepts that distinguish between and at the same time proclaim the continuity of the two phases in the history of God's plan for human salvation.

Within the box, then, are two complementary but separate accounts corresponding to two historical periods. Christians read the later one as an account of the "new" covenant handed on to them by Jesus that supersedes and fulfils the "old" covenant between God and Moses. This occurred partly as a response to Marcion's mid second-century proposal (then dubbed heretical) to substitute a Christian Gospel and Apostle (abbreviated-Luke and Paul) for the Jewish Torah and Prophets. It enabled and still enables Christians to retain as their own the Jewish texts that were, after all, Holy Scripture to Jesus.

However, the retention of the Jewish texts did more than solve the immediate problem with Marcion. It also allowed early Christian writers, communities and interpreters to relegate to the past those parts of the Old Testament that were problematic for them while retaining those that could be taken to prefigure salvation through Christ. Through this process they created what came to be known as the Christian canon: an authoritative collection of biblical texts shaped by and chosen to meet the needs of the early church communities. The canon emerged from those communities after a long and sometimes painful struggle to articulate their identity, and thereafter functioned as an instrument of authority, stability, and continuity in the lives of communities by setting them within the broader context of salvation history.

We can see this process already at work in the Gospels. In the story of Jesus and the Samaritan woman, for instance, her several affirmations of him as Savior are introduced by her query whether he is the "prophet who is to come." This no doubt refers to the promise of such a prophet in Deuteronomy 18:18, a text she might plausibly quote, since the first five books of the Jewish Scriptures constituted the Samaritan canon. But her query as to the coming of the Messiah and Jesus' claim to be that Messiah both lie outside the remit of that canon, for they hark back to the testimony of John the Baptist's disciples in an earlier passage in John's Gospel – the announcement that they have "found the Messiah" (John 1:42). Similarly the later testimony of other Samaritans that "we know this is the Savior of the world" (John 4:42) alludes to Jesus' earlier statement that "salvation is from the Jews" (John 4:22).

Over the first four centuries of Christianity, then, the Christian canon evolved through the need to move beyond a scriptural record comprised solely of the Jewish canon, and through struggles with heresy. The process was given added impetus by Constantine's urging the churches to achieve uniformity and so establish the authority of Christian writings throughout the Roman Empire. As part of the process, in 384 CE Pope Damasus charged Jerome, the prototypical Christian translator, to produce from the Greek originals a uniform and dependable text in Latin to supersede the variant Latin texts then in circulation. Whenever and by whoever the work was done, it is clear that the chosen texts were studied, interpreted and translated within the context of salvation history.

Today the results of that process can be seen – to use Segundo's graphic imagery – as grabbing hold of Jesus and boxing him within such universal categories (recall chapter three above, especially p.29f). The precise contents of the box, selected according to the needs and aspirations of early church communities, were later modified by still other groups who had varying aims. Within western Christianity different sets of books have become identified as the Roman Catholic canon, the Protestant canon, or even the Lutheran canon. In each case, the ultimate deciding factor has been the concern of a particular group as to how, or indeed whether Jesus as Savior is prefigured or figures within it. Thus, for example, Luther took the Epistle of James out of the box on the grounds that it did not mention Jesus – though his real reason may have been its deprecation of Pauline teaching.

Yet in spite of this and other incontrovertible evidence of human agency, it has generally been assumed that both the box of salvation history and the books that fit within it were constructed by God. Indeed that assumption has been the ultimate, unassailable referent for the authority of the canon. In 1932 Shaw remarked that there was a law on the English statute books that no statesman dared repeal, one that made it a felony "to question the scientific truth and *supernatural authority* of any word of Holy Scripture, the penalties extending to ruinous outlawry."[2] No doubt Shaw smiled at this twentieth-century legal absurdity. But did the "supernatural author" laugh?

As for the box itself, proponents have cited Augustine to demonstrate that its divine Architect had to reconstruct the original "box" – that is, the structure of meaning inherent in the Jewish canon – in order to accommodate the Christian doctrine of "original sin." Christians now read, study, interpret, and preach the biblical texts largely in the light of this hypothetical reconstruction; and this despite the obvious fact that, as Chilton Callaway observes, the Christian understanding of salvation history may not and often cannot reflect the authors' intentions.

This interpretive grid has therefore done much more than confine Jesus within a box of human presuppositions. Though statutory punishments may no longer apply, fundamentalist Christians have long proclaimed that the box and its chosen contents came directly from the divine maker's hand. God's view and knowledge of the whole of earth's history is, supposedly, shrink-wrapped within it. Every liturgical reading that is authenticated with the phrase, "This is the Word of the Lord" invokes and reinforces that assumed divine authority. And so God too is presumed to be "boxed" within human words, aspirations, story lines, texts, concepts, interpretations, and timescales. A great – and laughable – presumption, indeed.

The multifaceted canonizing process that has made this presumption possible is one that demanded and still demands decisions about both exclusion and inclusion – whether of books, passages or images. The intended result is to provide both a coherent interpretation of the context in which a Christian community finds itself today and a viable identity for it within that context. For part of the canon's function is to provide authoritative principles of interpretation by which a believing community can address its needs both to confirm and critique its established ethos. This internal critical function was at work when *Our God Has No Favorites* was written, and is evident in the kind of interpretations offered there and in previous chapters here in the hope of addressing the present needs of Christian ecumenism. The fact that those interpretations failed to have any noteworthy impact on church institutions demonstrates how strong is the drive towards maintaining a community's identity by exclusion.

But a certain kind of inclusion also needs to be challenged. The appropriation and compartmentalizing of the Jewish scriptures within the Christian canon too often resulted in negating their integrity: hence disparaging Judaism itself while at the same time implicitly disavowing the Jewishness of Jesus. Increased awareness of these consequences may lead us at last to abandon the term "Judaeo-Christian" when referring to Christian religious history. It is encouraging to note that lengthy discussions between Jewish and Christian scholars about what to call the Holy Scripture of the Jews led the editors of the latest edition of the German theological encyclopaedia *Religion in Geschichte und Gegenwart*[3] to agree that both "Hebrew Bible" and "Old Testament" should be used as standard terms throughout the encyclopaedia. And as one element of a theology after Auschwitz, a number of theologians and biblical scholars have begun to refer to the Jewish Scriptures as the First Testament, and the Christian canon as the Second Testament. This is the terminology that I shall use from here on.

These initiatives and their disclosure of underlying problems about the content of the Christian canon become especially important when the dominant paradigm for reading and interpreting it is a hypothetical "divine plan" of salvation. Although explicitly invoked in fundamentalist readings of the Bible, it is so widely implicit that Christians generally find it difficult to perceive, let alone to challenge, the latent antisemitism it supports. Internal Christian relationships are also jeopardized when besides claiming authority to provide or withhold salvation, certain people presume to declare what books are to be included in or excluded from the Bible, and even what translations and interpretations of them are to be used.

Eugene Nida, who has spent his life working with translators for the Bible Societies, has some interesting things to say about this. For some translators, he says, the acceptance or rejection of a particular Greek text depends not on its closeness to the original autographs, but on its agreement with such translations as the King James Version that have become more or less sacrosanct. Other translators, he says, turn textual scholarship on its head by insisting that the Greek text of the Jewish Scripture must be selected on the basis of its supposed support for such cherished doctrines as the trinity, the virgin birth, the deity of Jesus, and the inerrancy of the Scriptures. (Though Nida does not mention it, we see the same selection process at work in the contemporary fundamentalist condemnation of homosexuality.) In such cases the validity of a text is determined by its doctrinal content rather than doctrines being derived from Scripture.

Furthermore, Nida points out, over the years the Vulgate Latin text of Jerome — whether rendered by the English of the Douai translation or the King James Version (always accorded a capital letter), the Reina Valera in Spanish, or the Luther Bible in German — has become essentially canonical in the minds of many people. Still, he notes, the acceptance of any text as authoritative and canonical depends most upon its endorsement by ecclesiastical authorities or its publication by a well-known Bible Society. To show how even advertisers can contribute a measure of authority to a text, he quotes the advertisement for the King James Version that urges, "Read the Bible God reads."[4]

Does this make God laugh?

### Outside the box

So how do we get outside the canonical box? The first step is to become aware of its historical nature and to see it for what it is: a human construction based on human hypotheses. Then, looking more closely at its construction, we must recognize its potential for legitimating conflict with those excluded by it. This means becoming aware of its capacity for spiritual and physical exclusion — a function summed up in the damning slogan, "Outside the church [whichever paper one it is] there is no salvation."

And once outside, who do we find there? All the usual suspects. Those anathematized because of their heresies, their religious beliefs, their life choices, their politics or their sexual orientation. They have, so to speak, been evicted from the box. But what about those who never made it inside the box at all — those of all other faiths, many of which predate Christianity? And what of followers of faith systems that emerged after Christianity — notably Muslims or neo-pagans who are commonly perceived not only as outsiders but all too often as a threat to those inside? The number, status, and potential fate of fellow human beings whom Christians consider outsiders and treat accordingly is truly scandalous.

And finally, what of all those other beings in our more-than-human world who have never even been considered for insider status? They have been automatically excluded by us from the remit of the salvific relationships between God and the world that we have confined to and within human history.

"By us": if we have said them aloud and understood their force, those two words place us outside the box as well. For they shock us into awareness of its human rather than divine construction. This signals a shift in perception that enables us to think differently about ourselves. We begin to see human history within the context of earth's history, and ourselves dependent on the consistent and continuous relationships between organisms and their environments that constitute our world. And that in turn focuses our attention on what it means to be a member of the earth community.

It means, as I said in *Sacred Gaia*, that each of us is closely coupled with our environments and so contributes to continuous and consistent relationships between God and the world that can never be reduced to what we ourselves see and experience of that world, but that cannot be divorced from it either.[5] We realize then that the concept of salvation cannot be reduced simply to human redemption from human sin and its punishment, death. Nor is it to be seen as a posthumous award for good behavior during one's life on earth. It is its own reward, here and now, for living as a beneficial member of the earth community and contributing to the well-being of the thirsty, the hungry, the naked, the ill, the imprisoned, and the stranger in the land. This wider, deeper understanding of the concept recharges it with meanings such as wholeness, liberation, preservation, reclamation, and health. It too can be saved from fundamentalist shrinkage.

Once we get outside the canonical box, its sharp outlines and cutting edges gradually resolve into an earth-centered vision of ourselves and of God. In order to cultivate this perspective it is necessary to work through, in some detail, the outline of what I called, in *Apocalypse to Genesis*, an ecological paradigm or framework for a worldview.

### Inside an ecological paradigm

The first thing to be said about this worldview is that it admits of no notion of "outside." We and all other living beings, whether aware of it or not, whether we can describe it or not, are inside its practical remit. It encompasses what keeps us all alive. It is ecological because ecology as a practical scientific discipline is the study of organisms in their environments, their "homes." In fact, the root element "eco" (from the Greek *oikos)* means "house" or "home." While one organism and its "home" environment may be studied together as an ecosystem, it is clear that such an ecosystem is not isolated from others surrounding it, but is radically interconnected with them in the living whole we call Earth.

Therefore an ecological paradigm presupposes that all the ecosystems of the planet and the lives of the organisms they support are ultimately interconnected and interdependent. Making this oneness explicit in all its complexity and totality is the role of ecology as a philosophy. It recognizes that isolating the parts into separate systems, although essential for pragmatic purposes, can distort our understanding of both them and the whole. It also forbids us, as thinkers and as observers of that whole, to isolate ourselves from it in any meaningful way. We are part of it and affect it, not least by the questions we pose and the answers we expect.

This counteracts the tendency we have to relate to the world as detached observers who can separate it into discrete objects isolated from their larger contexts and from the observer's context also. By contrast, modern communications and systems theories such as are basic to the kind of ecological thinking advocated here work within a complex network of *metarelations* that can and do cross between contexts. This mode of thought is essential for dealing with the kind of global environmental problems we now face.

Of course, it is also essential for dealing with the network of metarelations between religions. In this instance it allows us to see those outside the Christian canonical box as integrally connected to those inside it. Life on earth is through and through relational, and interference at any one interface between religions like that we see in the Middle East today may have irreversible and unforeseen effects. Thinking outside the canonical box of Christianity and its cognitive defenses helps us see hypothetical boundaries between saved and heretic disappear in their sharing of and dependence on the same living space.

Using such ecological models enables us to respond to immediate problems by counteracting the results of previous bad solutions to immediate problems – bad precisely because of their destructive effects on the larger patterns surrounding the problem. A bad solution is one that has a single purpose or goal, such as increased production; or in the case of the "war on terror," eliminating terrorists without due concern for the soil – physical, economic, political, and religious – from which they have sprung. It is typical of such solutions (and we have seen this in the Iraq War of 2003) that they fail to achieve their purposes despite exorbitant expenditures of economic and social capital – and human life.

A good solution, on the other hand, is one in harmony with those larger patterns. It acts within them the way a healthy organ acts within the body. But a healthy organ does not – as the mechanistic approach would have us believe – *give* health to the body. It is not there to be exploited for the body's health, but is a composite part of that health. The health of organ and organism is one and the same, just as is the health of organism and ecosystem. Likewise, religious solutions offered by fundamentalist Christians today, because of their declared intention to limit them to the future salvation of a chosen few, cannot contribute to the health, well-being, or salvation of humanity as a whole.

The particular challenge posed by an ecological paradigm (and the source of its most exciting potential) is that it urges us to adopt a systemic approach to life through accepting the systemic structure of the individual human being, the systemic structure of the culture in which we live, and the systemic structure of the biological, political, and industrial systems that surround us. To this I would add the systemic structure of religious beliefs. As I will point out in the final chapter, with all these interconnections in mind, we may go on to recognize and be guided by the wisdom of the totally systemic creature James Lovelock named *Gaia* after the poetic ancient Greek word for the Earth.

We have no trouble, he says, with the idea that noble entities such as people are made up from an intricate interconnected set of cell communities. We don't find it too difficult to consider a nation or a tribe as an entity made up of its people and the territory they occupy. But what of large entities like ecosystems and Gaia? The breathtaking view of Earth from space at last gave us the personal sense of a living planet. The astonishing thing about this creature is its aliveness as it floats free in a dark void. We see swirling drifts of cloud cover and uncover the half-hidden masses of land, and if we could follow these latter shapes for a geological era or two, we would see the continents in motion as they glide across the molten rock beneath. This moon's eye view of the world has been made possible for us by space technology. We can never go back to a flat earth mentality now that we have made this leap in perception resulting from our detailed knowledge of the planet's life and motion.

But viewing this free-floating world from a point outside it might foster the dangerous impression that it is discrete from us and can be treated accordingly. Our very ability to visualize the larger entity of which we are a part can inhibit our ability to perceive ourselves as inseparable from it. The two perceptions must be kept in balance. Our inclination to analytic detachment has to be complemented by a conscious decision to keep the whole in view, and vice versa. And this is as true in religion as it is in ecology.

So what does an ecological paradigm look like?

### An ecological paradigm

Unlike Christianity's canonical "box" of salvation, the most notable feature of the ecological paradigm is that it denies "outsideness": there is lit-

erally no "where" and no "one" outside it. For an ecological paradigm presupposes a sense of belonging to a system that functions as a whole, no matter how small or large the particular system one is engaged with at any one
time. Thus it follows that one has at least an implicit awareness of the other
systems with which we interact and of their interaction with yet other ones.
This extension of awareness promotes workable solutions for environmental
problems. To use the example given earlier, it reminds us that a healthy
organ is one element of bodily health, and not a discrete object intended to
provide or be used for health.

The second notable feature of an ecological paradigm is the inescapable
inadequacy of my or anyone else's description of it. This has much to do
with the fact that I am attempting a theological and not a scientific analysis
of this worldview. Nevertheless, however exhaustive a description might be
fashioned in terms of any one discipline or author's expertise, one can never
describe all the relationships within a system. We are touching here on the
fundamental relationship between language and reality that by its very
nature makes all description of that reality relative to the whole truth about
it. The acceptance of this "learned ignorance" acts as an important counterweight to any scientific claim to total knowledge of earth's ecology.

Accepting this inadequacy in our interpretations is an important factor
in any human interaction with the world. Here it directs our attention to
another feature of the paradigm. Since our language is always going to be a
more or less inadequate attempt at conveying the truth about something,
then if our aim is to communicate perceptions or increase knowledge, it
helps to begin with an identifiable entity. Thus a leaf or a branch may represent the tree for us, or a whisker the cat. Yet while such images are properly used to represent the entity in question, they do no more than that.
Understanding the world by means of thought and then translating thoughts
into words is like trying to make out the contours of a cave with the aid of
a small flashlight casting a bright but very thin beam.

The rock we focus on is not the cave. The leaf is not the tree. The
whisker not the cat. The map not the territory. Furthermore, any representa-
tion necessarily excludes those features which make any entity unique. Only
in the night of the imagination are all cats black. This gap between what we
perceive, what we mean, and what we say lies at the heart of theological language. As well as keeping us dissatisfied with what we say, the gap keeps us
constantly on the lookout for better images, better representations, and
more precise modes of speech. Therefore another feature of the ecological

paradigm is its pressure on us to keep the pathways to other systems, mentally, linguistically, and physically open, and to learn from them how to see familiar features in a new way.

This is important not only for language; indeed it is vital for sustaining the life of any system – including the one we call Christianity – and for its evolution. Lack of input, of stimulus, and of energy are all symptoms of a closed system that atrophies for want of interaction with those around it. This is precisely the danger we face when we box in Jesus by accepting the presuppositions of canonical salvation history. In contrast to this, an eco- logical paradigm demands openness at all the junctions between the pri- mary system and those accessible to it; at the intersecting pathways that vitalize and revitalize that system by conveying exchanges of information and energy. Obviously this is not one-way traffic, for a flow of vitality from the home system to those connected with it results in a two-way exchange that affects both the part and the whole.

Using pathways to systems other than our own in order to learn from them is both easier and harder for us than it used be, for while the media do much to make other places and cultures accessible, the very superficial- ity of their communication keeps us from entering into those systems in any real way. This is another example of the "moon's eye view of the world" problem. The familiar "nearness" of the television screen can all too readily distance us from what is projected on it. Becoming a spectator can encour- age disengagement rather than commitment.

Once again, however, an allied feature of the paradigm acts as a safe- guard. We learn to recognize openings to larger systems previously unknown but truly important for us. On a personal note, this has happened to me as a result of Gaia theory opening up the field of earth system science within which I now see my life – including my religious life. One crucial aspect of this recognition is appropriateness: what could be more appropriate than to understand why I'm alive at this moment and what sustains my life (or does not sustain it) here and now? Another crucial aspect of becoming open to this field of understanding is its fruitfulness: it enables me, however mini- mally, to recognize what is life-enhancing and what is not. Both these insights have helped me see "my" salvation as inextricably linked to the enhancement and well-being of all life on earth, at all times and everywhere.

This links up with yet another element in the paradigm. The pathways we plot and consciously maintain are only part of the whole territory. They are affected by things that have gone on (such as the formation of the bibli- cal canon) and that are going on now even though they do not involve me in any recognizable way. Awareness of this extra-personal dimension can prevent us from mistaking the part of life we are involved with for the whole, and warns us to leave the way open for information to come down pathways as yet unperceived. Just think how greatly our understanding of the Christian canon has been enriched by the discovery of "extra-canonical" texts at Qumran and Nag Hammadi.

Keeping these factors in mind can help one develop an important attitude I call "ecological humility." This and its close relationship to the theological modesty proper to saying anything about God will be discussed at some length in chapter ten. The practical function of this form of humility is to remind us that we can never gather all relevant information, much less retain it; and this recognition keeps us from absolutism in identifying problems, proposing solutions, or defining positions. The temptation to absolutize besets us all, and as we have seen, is endemic in Christianity.

Taking all these features of an ecological paradigm together, the overarching effect is that of openness within constraints, an openness that presupposes we not only accept intellectually the interactive nature of our own and other ecosystems, but that also invites us to respond to it in a way that fosters healthy interactions between organism, society and the total systemic creature we call world. Most important, it makes us aware of and attentive to the interdependent character of relationships in which things are ultimately intelligible only in terms of each other. Each is seen as part of an immense complexity of subtly balanced relationships that, like an endless knot, has no loose end from which it can be untangled and put in supposed order. Or to change the metaphor to one better known: no one of us is an island. We are all part of the mainland — and of the sea surrounding it.

Myriad examples of Christian exclusionary practice testify that these apparently simple ecological rules have not been kept. Systems have been treated as though they exist in isolation; pathways to other systems have been blocked; available information has not been taken into account. Worse yet, no compensation is made for the fact that individual human consciousness, which is necessarily partial or even distorted, has often been taken as the measure of the whole. Theologically more serious are the obvious and immodest effects of taking human consciousness as commensurate with divine consciousness.

The need to change to an ecological paradigm is increasingly evident in a world beset by global environmental and political disasters. The need for change is equally evident within a religious earthscape in which traditional Christianity has behaved largely as a closed system of human salvation. It has treated the surrounding systems of philosophy, art, science, and other religions as though they could offer little or nothing of value. Worse yet, such paradigmatic insights as those of Galileo and Darwin were attacked for challenging knowledge deemed available only to the closed Christian system. To a large extent, it has closed off its sacred system of worship within church walls and shut out the perception of sacredness in the land beneath and beyond them. The central chapters of *Sacred Gaia* explore in detail how this self-blinding dynamic has legitimated and reinforced the disastrous expansion of technological exploitation of our planet's resources promoted by the cultural offshoot of Christianity known as modern western capitalism.

The following chapter takes a look inside the canonical box from an ecological perspective, and thereby enables me to pinpoint the damaging effects of Christianity's exclusionary power on women and on Nature.

# 6

# Ecofeminism and Canon

E
ven before we take that closer look at the contents of the canonical box, it is important to note that its original construction and subsequent decisions about what to keep inside it have been an exclusively male enterprise. Like the banquet in the rabbinic parable mentioned at the beginning of the last chapter, only men participate. Predictably enough, this state of affairs has long escaped most men's attention — or if their attention was drawn to it, they generally appealed to the contents of the box in order to justify it. Throughout the twentieth century however, as women were increasingly allowed to study and even to teach theology (note the condescension involved), this gender deficit has increasingly been taken into account. As a consequence, attention has focused on two of its most obvious effects: the almost complete lack of feminine imagery for God in Christian religious discourse and the near absence of women from any public ecclesiastical office or liturgical role. That Shaw took up these issues on his own initiative and in his own inimitable fashion shows that some men have felt it a matter of simple justice to speak out on them.

At the same time, women in such other disciplines as philosophy, anthropology, language studies and some of the sciences have become increasingly critical of the patriarchal nature of western culture: of the pervasive religious and social perception of men as inherently superior to women and hence rightfully more powerful. These women have devoted their energies to raising awareness of the exclusion of feminine consciousness from all patriarchal systems in which the male norm and the human norm are presumed to be identical. This work continues through patient and difficult deconstruction of gender inequalities and their effects wherever and however they occur.

As a result there has emerged a particular link between cultural conceptions about women and those about Nature, one particularly evident in metaphorical language and in constellations of behavior towards them both.[1] From a growing recognition of this linkage has emerged a synthesis of ecology and feminism known as ecofeminism. It is a philosophical endeavor to clarify and bring into focus the interconnections between the domination of women and the abusive exploitation of Nature. It works by bringing an ecological paradigm into play while employing a feminist perspective. From a variety of theoretical positions it sets out to disclose the intrinsic link in male-dominated cultures between how one speaks about women and Nature and how one behaves towards them.

In the present chapter I shall first highlight this linkage by looking more closely at the contents of the Christian canonical box, and then assess its function in legitimizing the almost total exclusion of women's experience from those contents and, by default, from the realm of practical and spiritual power. In the following chapters this critique will lead to a positive outcome in the form of a transformative interpretation of the opening chapters of Genesis — an exposition based on what the text actually says rather than on what has been read into it within the context of traditional salvation history.

### What is the canon?

The particular form the canon now takes was discussed in some detail in the previous chapter. Its existence in this form has up to now largely been taken for granted. Indeed that notional and practical assent to its existence has meant that it appears to be an integral part of the Christian landscape, indeed one of its fundamental contours. When women began examining its foundations, however, they noted that the accumulation of texts, interpretations, inferences, decrees and hypotheses that they found had been deposited there over the centuries by men only. Since these compilers long used the ecclesiastical term "the deposit of faith" to describe this accumulation, the question of who made the deposit has until recently gone largely unasked.

The perceived range of its influence as the statutory list of authoritative Christian texts was spelt out in a fifth century definition of the canon as "that which has been believed everywhere, always, and by all."[2] This notion of an all-inclusive Christian norm prevails up to the present day and rests on the assumption that the Bible as we have it now (with or without certain

writings of the church Fathers and conciliar pronouncements, and in whatever translation we presently favor) was directly inspired by God – and that
Christians everywhere have always believed this. While the universalist
aspect of the claim has clearly proved unsustainable, the more particular
assertion that the canon defines the contents of belief for *Christians everywhere and at all times* still remains widely accepted.

This claim rests on the allied Christian presupposition that the interpretation of the statutory texts is definitively propounded through the authority of the Spirit and handed on (*traditio*) from one generation of men to the
next. The exclusion of some books from the Protestant canon and their
inclusion by the Catholic hierarchy does not repudiate the notion of canon
but rather reinforces it, since both actions were claims of authority to define
what it means to be Christian – within a particular paper church. However,
the ordinary believer, unconcerned with the finer points of ecclesiastical
government, usually takes for granted that the books of the Bible as printed
in a particular edition constitute the basic written record of God's revelation
to the founding fathers of whatever church she or he belongs to.

It is true that up to the time of the Second Vatican Council, although
the Roman Catholic Church taught that there were two distinct sources of
revelation, *Scripture* and the recorded authorized interpretations collectively
known as *Tradition*, in practice the emphasis was on tradition. In 1965 however, the Council's document on revelation devoted its two opening chapters to revelation and its transmission but without explicitly distinguishing
them as separate sources. Four of the six chapters in the document deal
expressly with the Bible – in which, the document says, God revealed himself to men, spoke to men out of the abundance of his love and invited them
into fellowship with himself. By this revelation the deepest truth about God
and the salvation of man is made clear to us in Christ. After speaking in
many places and various ways through the prophets, God last of all has spoken to us by his Son, the Word made flesh, sent "as a man to men."[3]

The patriarchal imagery in this statement offers but one example of why
ecofeminists object to the inappropriate identification of the male with the
whole of humanity. It also reiterates the point made in the last chapter about
the contents of the canon being handed on in the "box" of salvation history
from one generation of men to the next. The Protestant position in regard
to the revelation of God was concisely stated by Karl Barth. He described
Holy Scripture as an entity that stands superior in order to the church, temporal like it, yet different from it. This is because it is the canon of the
church, that is, the regulation, the pattern, what is fixed in the church as
authoritative. From the fourth century on, he says, the word "canon" has

developed into the list of books in the Bible recognized in the church as apostolic and therefore authoritative.[4]

Both the Roman Catholic and Protestant statements define the status and role of the Christian canon in its contemporary form. What I want to focus on here is the relationship between its contents and the universalist claim — made by church authorities with respect to both time and place — that has made it appear to be an unchanging contour in the Christian landscape and a fundamental fact: accepted by everyone within it as a constitutive strategic and stabilizing feature that orients their vision of God and their way of living.

## The nature of the contents

Uncovering its contents and function literally uncovers the ground on which this prominent feature of Christianity rests. It is the land occupied by predominantly Mediterranean peoples living before the fifth century. It is no surprise, then, to find an obviously patriarchal religious structure ruling the hierarchical cultures of these people. Those among them who belonged to the ruling classes by virtue of birth, literacy and learning or ecclesiastical position assumed they had power to choose and to interpret the contents of the canonical box. Also, they successfully claimed that that power was given them "from above": from the Spirit handed on by Jesus to certain men, the apostles, who in turn handed that power on to others. Then as now the authority to interpret the Scriptures definitively was attributed to the highest level of church government, from which and on which all other powers depend.

A corollary to this is that the power of the Spirit is assumed to be confined within and by hierarchical relationships. Thus hierarchical churches either explicitly or implicitly claim to be not simply the occasion and context for salvation and its beneficial effects but the primary or even sole source of salvation itself. Jesus' intimation of the nature of God's Spirit — that like the wind it is free to act how when and where it pleases — is repudiated. It too is "boxed" in within church walls; assumed to be possessed by certain men; dispensed or withheld at their discretion. From these presuppositions emerge such scandalously presumptuous statements as "outside the church there is no salvation."

So we find small elite male groups living in a particular time, place and culture defining the scope and power of their choice of canonical texts — and in the process establishing and confirming their own power. Taking a closer look at those texts, we see that they likewise arose from eastern Mediterranean cultures, most of them over a period of at least a thousand years preceding the formation of the canon. That being the case, how balanced a view of the world can we expect to find in them? As the product of a small literate minority within a largely illiterate culture, they necessarily represent the views of that dominant minority. How balanced a view of life do they offer modern people? How relevant are ancient texts that reflect the views of an elite minority to the lives of today's Christians the world over?

One of the most forthright and, it must be said, uncomplimentary assessments of their possible relevance comes from the biblical scholar Andrew Hunter. Observing the ethical "misfits" between our culture and that of the biblical world, he finds good grounds for asserting that the world of the Bible has more in common with contemporary Afghanistan under the Taliban than with Britain or North America. He cites the Bible's assumptions about women, gay men, ethnic minorities, blasphemy, slavery, war and capital punishment as being offensive to every inclusive-minded Christian.[5]

It is hardly surprising then that ecofeminists refuse to take the canonical record of relationships between God and the world as representative of the whole truth about how to live well now. They also refuse to read its contents within the traditional box of human salvation history. By doing so they refuse to accept as God's will the continuance of patriarchal power structures that it enshrines and that church authorities adduce as legitimation for the subordination of women. For this misappropriation has ensured that women's voices have been omitted from the ongoing interpretive process and that an exclusionary view of the more-than-human community has been canonized. Therefore ecofeminist theologians claim the right to include women's experience as critical in the process of reinterpreting biblical traditions in ways that contribute to the well-being of the entire earth community.

### Digging deeper

Starting from this premise, the contents of the supposedly universal canon raise some obvious questions. Why these texts and not others? Who decided that those chosen constituted the only revealed truth about God's dealings with the world? On what grounds was it decided that Augustine's interpretation of them within the context of salvation history should be canonized?

In asking why these texts and not others, it is important to note that the oldest deposit, the Hebrew Bible, comes from sources removed both hierarchically and demographically from the lives of most Israelites. This is hardly surprising since in a largely pre-literate or illiterate society the keeping of records was necessarily confined to certain classes. The Pentateuch, that part of the canon most concerned with human relationships with the land, is by and large the product of priestly, all-male, hereditary groups whose leadership was largely concentrated in the Temple at Jerusalem. Virtually the entire historiographic account – the so-called Deuteronomic history that runs from Joshua through to Kings and constitutes the core of the Hebrew Bible – is generally understood to be based on court records or traditions circulating in royal circles. The post-exilic chronicles were similarly compiled at the behest of clerical governors like Ezra and Nehemiah.

Two points are at issue here: the first is that these attributions, whether or not they were literary devices, led to the common acceptance of these writings as authoritative. The second is that their origin among the official ruling classes, whether royal, priestly or gubernatorial, necessarily excluded the views of most men and certainly those of the majority of Israelite women. Therefore, although the governing establishment was unrepresentative of the population as a whole, yet the experience of the male rulers of Israel has been and still is taken to represent the whole history of God's relationship with this people.[6]

This is equally true of those texts written after the death of Jesus. Paul's education and the evangelists' literary skills were important factors in the acceptance of their writings as normative. Paul was a city person. The city breathes through his language. Even when he uses metaphors such as olive trees or gardens, the fluent Greek evokes the schoolroom more than the farm; he is more at home with the clichés of Greek rhetoric, drawn from gymnasium, stadium or workshop. Depending on the city for his education and an essentially urban trade for his livelihood, he had little sensitivity for farm workers, whether slave or free, or for the few whose wealth and status depended on their agricultural estates. When Paul rhetorically catalogues the places where he has suffered danger, he divides the world into city, wilderness and sea (2 Cor 11:26). His world does not include the *chora*, the productive countryside; outside the city there is nothing – *eremia*. Since his world in effect consisted only of the cities of the Roman Empire, he makes the extraordinary claim that since from Jerusalem all the way to Illyricum he has fully preached the Gospel of Christ, he need no longer work in these regions (Rom 15:19). What he had actually done was to plant small cells of Christians in scattered households in some of the strategically located cities of the northeastern part of the-Mediterranean basin.[7]

The authors of the Gospel records may or may not have included a countryman. Popular attribution ascribes them to a physician (Luke), a philosopher-theologian (John), a Hellenistic catechist (Matthew) and a disciple of Peter's who made his way to Rome and became recorder of the community there (Mark). Whoever they were, their accounts concentrate almost exclusively on what is commonly called the "public" life of Jesus — activities set primarily in towns and cities — and on his debates with the ruling classes in the context of his trial and death at the hands of spiritual and imperial elites.

The Pauline Epistles and Acts record Paul's own battles with these as well as with the male ruling council of the emerging church (cf. 1 Cor 11:3, 5; 14:34f.). Attribution to him was enough for the so-called Pastoral Letters to be considered authoritative, especially where they lay down rules for the "normative" relationships within church hierarchies — for example, regulations that exclude women from spiritual authority. The pseudo-Pauline first letter to Timothy goes so far as to offer a grossly distorted interpretation of Genesis in its attempt to justify the male right to exclude (1 Tim 2:11–14). This appeal to a flawed male hermeneutic of Genesis was to have lasting consequences for the role of women within Christianity.

The already noted proclivity of Christian writers to employ dubious scriptural interpretations to reinforce later religious and cultural assumptions must be seen for what it is: a literary and rhetorical device. Then the internal dialogue in the Second Testament between the Hebrew Bible and the nascent Christian community can be seen as an important aspect of the ecclesiastical system of reinforcing interpretive authority. The Christian canon is certainly not a master code possessing the ability to present us with unambiguous "divine" truth. Recognizing this, we see that the Pauline emphasis on the authority of Jesus as Lord may be a vital personal insight but it cannot be used to argue for a universal relationship with God that takes precedence over all others.

### The partial nature of the canon

From an ecofeminist theological viewpoint, priests, prophets, kings, officers, bureaucrats and apostles are seen for what they were: small elite male groups within population masses composed of both males and females who all, we may suppose, had a relationship with their creator God. The biblical concentration on these elites to the exclusion of the rest of the people has necessarily given us a partial vision of our religious origins — one that has taken such controlling minorities out of their original contexts and made them appear representative of the whole. This goes some way towards answering the question about which records were kept and which discarded. However numerically small these groups were, they had enormous power and influence, not least because of their ability to articulate and record the meaning of their relationship with God and with the world around them.

Therefore their ideologies, that is, their religious understanding of events and ideas came to be considered normative. Not only that, but once accepted, these doctrines also became the apparent divine norm and hence the unassailable basis for such social and religious structures as monarchy and ecclesiastical hierarchy. The most important response to this arrogation of authority is to recognize and insist on the relative status of these writings. We also need to analyze the power structures that enabled them to be circulated and accepted as normative — a situation surprisingly analogous to that found within academic and ecclesiastical institutions today.

We must also keep in mind the theologians collectively known as "Church Fathers," who since the second century CE have maintained the dominance of "orthodox" interpretations of these writings over the Christian imagination. They shared a Greek culture and transmitted their teaching through the concepts and categories of Greek philosophy. They also shared the reverence for Scriptural authority manifest in the Christian records written after Jesus' death. Thus when the late fifth century author of *The Celestial Hierarchy* wanted to give his vision authority, he adopted the pseudonym "Denys the Areopagite" by way of claiming authorship as the Denys who was Paul's first convert in Athens. Since Athens then meant philosophy, and more precisely Plato, Denys the Athenian convert stands at the point where Christ and Plato meet. The pseudonym expressed the author's belief that the truths that Plato grasped belonged to Christ and therefore need not be abandoned when embracing faith in Christ.[8] This view was shared by some of the most influential shapers of the Christian tradition.

Returning to the Israelite stage of the tradition, we must recall that those who shaped it were not only exclusive in terms of gender, number and education. They were separated from most of their fellow Israelites in that as residents of Jerusalem or of other major cities, they participated in an urban pattern of life. All these factors are important for an assessment of the effects of those texts that they included or excluded. Their androcentric bias and urban elite orientation mean that even the information they appear to offer about agrarian life may misrepresent it. The highly stylized Leviticus texts, for instance, cannot be taken as universally applicable norms with respect to women, animals and agricultural practices.[9] Indeed, within the Christian canon a notable outburst is attributed to God, no less, who forcefully repudiates such stereotyping by insisting to Peter that no creature created by God can be classified as unclean (Acts 10:13–15).

Along with a partiality toward urban society, a deprecation of the agricultural way of life has been hard-wired into the Christian interpretation of the biblical sources in all sorts of covert ways. Until recently, biblical archaeology concentrated disproportionately on the urban sites most likely to provide verification or illumination of the political history recorded in the Bible. Consequently the sites chosen tended to be major cities assumed to have been cultic and administrative centers. Archaeologists concentrated on fortification systems, palaces, villas, and public buildings. In so doing, they chose features of urban life related to the military, to the governing elite and to the cultic establishment. This contributed still further to the lack of visibility of the middle and lower echelons of society and of all those whose realm of activity was oriented to private or domestic affairs. Insofar as women's lives were typically confined to the domestic realm, biblical archaeology has offered virtually nothing that could be used to reconstruct the social or religious role of women — or for that matter anyone belonging to the non-urban, non-elite or non-specialist segments of the population.[10] In short, the records offer almost nothing from which we can glean a balanced understanding of early Israelite society or of the "ordinary" person's relationship with God.

The same invisibility cloaks the life of the early Christian communities, but it is often compensated for by academic reconstructions of sites associated with the life and death of Jesus. The imperial basilicas of the Christian Diaspora have long been studied for clues to the presuppositions and precepts of Christian worship. By the late second century, the episcopal model of leadership had developed into an urban hierarchy in which the bishop became the presiding pastor at the major congregation of the city and supervised others. The pattern of episcopal hierarchy expanded in the next two centuries into provincial and imperial forms by which the presiding bishops of major sees supervised bishops and elders under them. Gradually, the church began to duplicate the political structures of the late Roman Empire and to construct an ecclesiastical counterpart to the Roman system of urban and provincial governors.[11]

In such ways, the very notion of church became identified with visible structures designed and built by men and church membership became synonymous with attendance at ceremonies within them. As a consequence, only those who go out of their homes to worship were and still are counted as "the Church."

### Effects of the canon on women and on attitudes to the earth

One obvious effect of this Christian stereotyping was that the home, woman-centered in its rituals of bringing forth and nourishing life, became desacralized. Instead of ritualizing natural birth through the water and blood of the mother, baptism in church became the religious rite by which one denigrates one's natural life – a gift derived from and nourished by the waters of the mother's womb, but according to Augustine's dismal postulate, contaminated by "original sin" at the moment of conception. Therefore the child must undergo a "rebirth" through "holy" water blessed by hierarchically appointed men. Even if a particular church baptizes only adults, it thus alienates women's experience of life-giving from the sacred and excludes it from canonical recognition. Instead of integrating mother and child into a group representing the whole of humankind, baptismal ritual presupposes a religious community that sees itself as separate from the natural order of life.

The same distancing process occurs in regard to the nourishment and sustaining of life. Women's continuous experience of lifegiving centers on the nurture and growth of their families through the gathering and preparation of food shared at meals. The central symbolic act of sharing food within Christianity, the Eucharist, has been radically alienated from its natural setting (one that Jesus would have been familiar with) by being literally taken out of women's hands and confined to a church sanctuary. There the symbolic act of blessing and giving food and drink has been "elevated" into a symbol of the power to control divine life, a power that the clergy claim to possess in a way that is beyond the access of "natural" human beings.[12]

This tendency to reserve ceremonial power in churches to those males seen as sole possessors of the Spirit has contributed much to the Christian desacralizing of attitudes to "ordinary" food, a point made in chapters two, three and four above. I discuss the further theological and ecological implications of this at some length in *Sacred Gaia* and again in *Gaia's Gift*. An ecologically paradigmatic Christianity would seek to heal the division between Eucharist and home by restoring a sense of the sacred to every meal, and by re-valuing women's traditional role in handing on the blessing of life, a gift offered and sustained by the lives and deaths of other beings within the earth community.

The early bias toward imposing metropolitan church buildings incorporated an important shift not only in the perception of home but also of the earth. Special man-made edifices became isolated sanctuaries dedicated to the "supernatural"; holy places dotted about a natural supposedly profane world. The sacred was sequestered within walls made with men's hands. Human activities were classified as "holy" or "profane" according to whether or not they took place within a "consecrated" place. One stepped outside such a place, therefore, into a world that was not sacred. The accepted rea-

Garden myth

son for the "profanity" of Nature was that it had become corrupted through
Adam's sin.[13] But whereas humanity might be redeemed within these build-
ings through baptism into Christ (the second Adam), outside them "fallen"
Nature remained unredeemed.

Adam
↓
Eve

In such ways the foundations were laid for a dualistic modeling of
Christian society into two kinds of activity, the private and the public, that
came to be seen as corresponding to the profane and the sacred. The private domestic sphere revolved around home and field and the reproductive
processes centered on women and the natural world. While not explicitly
excluded from the realm of the sacred, the home ceased to be its primary
locus. The public sphere was everything outside the home environment:
collective rituals, legal or judicial regulation of supradomestic matters, and
official worship.

Theologically as well as culturally, then, female identity was linked with
the domestic and male identity with the public. Women were associated
with "natural" functions occurring in domestic contexts, men were more
closely identified with public functions.[14] Consciously and unconsciously,
the domestic female habitat, whether of humankind or beast, was linked
with the profane, and the male public sphere was the area of encounter with
the sacred. In regard to the more-than-human world, any possibility of locat-
ing the divine there was implicitly denied.

Today it is official Christian teaching that Nature is desacralized – that
is, "fallen."[15] And even those encouraging religious mysticism, R. C.
Zaehner for example, tell us that it means a total and absolute detachment
from Nature, from *"all that is not God."*[16] Yet hardly a day goes by without
concerned persons reminding us that unless we recover a sense of reverence
for Nature, we are not likely to devote the necessary energy and resources
to repairing the harm we have done to it. How is this sense to be rediscov-
ered in a tradition that has consistently denied Nature's right to reverence
for its own sake because it has lost the perception of the primal relationship
between the sacred and the more-than-human world?

Part of the answer, I submit, is to look very closely at canonical interpretations of texts on which such views of women and Nature have been
predicated, and to determine how they can and ought to be revised in the
light of an ecological paradigm. One such examination is offered in the next
chapter.

# 7

# Genesis within the Box

One common perception of the opening chapters of Genesis is that they recount a hierarchical process of creation, and that they both establish and conform to a basic order in which different types of being are graded according to their position relative to those above them. In the religious hierarchy implicit in the Genesis text, God naturally occupies the top position; accordingly, those of most value are presumed closest to God and those of least value the furthest away. Just as in political hierarchies whose summit is occupied by a sovereign or president, the religious model takes the form of a pyramid, with increasing numbers towards its base. And for the masses assigned to that station, their distance from the top renders them lowest in prestige and power. Christian hierarchy relegates the earth and its more-than-human inhabitants to that lowly status, while members of our own species are understood to be nearest to God – indeed, just below the angelic choirs.

While no chief executive would claim divine appointment or cite God as his immediate patron, the Christian model of hierarchy has been sanctified by the doctrine of its divine establishment. This presupposes conformity to its demands from all within it. The late-fifth century Christian mystic and Neo-Platonist Denys the Areopagite – whom we met in the last chapter – apparently coined the word *hierarchia* from the Greek words *hieros* (sacred) and *arche* (rule or order). He used it in working out a cosmic pattern of government – a "holy order" comprised of low, middle, and high dispensations of being and action – and successive levels of divine knowledge and spiritual activity that stretch from the lowest (on earth) to the highest (in heaven). Thinking about the world in this way entails a complex of ideas and sub-ideas implicit in some of the discussions in previous chapters.

## Hierarchy and Genesis

It is now time to make them explicit, especially in regard to the Genesis account of God creating the world. First there is the idea that like the rest of the universe, Earth is an artifact fashioned by God from inert, corruptible matter. It is presumed to have had no definable shape or particular structure until the external power of God formed it from the primordial confusion of matter. One biblical image that directly conveys this idea is that of God as Potter. It suggests unintelligent inactive matter being shaped into various forms by intelligent active spirit: God as "Maker" of the universe. This matter, the "lowest" grade or state of being and incapable of spiritual or intelligent activity, is the very substance of earth. Its place within the sacred order is at the very bottom and furthest from God because it lacks any capacity to know God.

As this image of God the Creator assumed religious dominance it combined with Greek philosophy to reinforce the prevailing image of the human individual: a creature composed of flesh (matter), but animated by an indwelling spirit that exercises control over the body. This, of course, presupposes spiritual or intellectual power over matter, to form or de-form it as we will. And therefore this divine gift not only enables us to subdue and govern our personal "matter," our own flesh, but positively requires us to do so. As we read in the now rather quaint but religiously precise language of the Articles of Religion in the Book of Common Prayer, "The flesh lusteth always contrary to the spirit; and therefore in every person born into this world, it (flesh) deserveth God's wrath and damnation."[1]

Here let me enter the brief reminder that within an ecological paradigm we see ourselves rather differently. We know that we are not "made of" body and spirit, we *are* body and spirit; that a tree is not "made of" wood, a tree *is* wood; a mountain is not "made of" rock, it *is* rock. Taking this notion seriously means that strictly speaking the day of my birth was not the day I was "born into this world." That would suggest that before the elements constituting my flesh and spirit were, so to speak, "put together," I was not in the world. In fact, however, I did not come *into* the world but *out* of it – out of the ecosystems that sustained my parents and theirs before them.

But the hierarchical interpretations of the Genesis account do more than simply lead us to perceive of ourselves as "made of" spirit and body. The text also says that God designed every life form to "bring forth according to its kind" – that is, to be species-specific: acorns produce oaks, and tadpoles grow up to be frogs. This has fostered the idea that the different ways in which a tree is one thing and a frog another are governed by laws operating in obedience to the design of God their maker. The classification "according to their kind" also involves the three-fold Genesis model in which creation is divided into the earth, the waters and the firmament; and creatures live in and belong to one of the three elements of earth, water, or air.

Classification according to kind and according to element are combined in Genesis and in other biblical narratives as a way of distinguishing between "clean" and "unclean," "pure" and "polluted." The governing principle here, accepted as inherent in the divine order, is that "clean" animals conform fully to their class and behave properly according to their element. Therefore they "please" God and can be offered in sacrifice. "Unclean" species – those whose members do not so "con-form" or whose typology confounds the general scheme – do not, it is assumed, "please" God. They do not hop, jump, or walk upon the earth but creep, crawl, or "swarm" upon it. This distinction between clean and unclean in regard to pleasing God is explicitly invoked in the closing episode of the Noah story (Genesis 6–9). Nevertheless, as we have already noted, the God depicted in Peter's vision in Acts repudiates this whole scheme.

Genesis pictures the serpent as the archetypical "unclean" creature, "cursed" by God to crawl on the earth on its belly, to eat soil, and to be trodden under foot by the woman's offspring. The holiness codes in Leviticus also regard conformity in regard to kind and element as the ideal. To be "holy" is to be "whole" – to have an integrity that includes perfection of the individual being, both of kind and of the behavior that corresponds to that kind.[2]

This taxonomy according to class, element, and individual integrity is applied to the hierarchical grading of people no less than animals. Those who do not behave "according to their kind" – that is, according to an accepted and easily perceived religious, sexual or physical norm – are routinely devalued on the assumption that there is a divine principle that requires them to conform to such a norm. The inference of laws of appropriate behavior, whether attributed to Genesis or genetics, is used to legitimize such classification.

What God thinks of our grading systems or of our attempts to validate them in God's name is, of course, another matter. So is the opinion of those devalued by these criteria. But the sacrifice of human potential occasioned by such devaluation, as well as the oppression it promotes and justifies, are certainly not laughing matters – for ourselves or for God. Looking back over previous chapters, we can see how the assumptions behind them, although seldom made explicit, have helped give religious legitimacy to the exercise of Christian exclusionary power in relation to our fellow human beings. Being black, brown, disabled, homosexual, or religiously non-conformist in behavior or beliefs has served to sanction not only an individual's exclusion from a community or hierarchical office, but her or his active persecution. And our assumption of absolute power over all "brute" species on the grounds of their lack of soul or spirit has led to such dire consequences for them as would surely make the God of Job weep.

### Genesis and ecology

These canonical religious and cultural accretions that function in such unhealthy ways make it all the more necessary to look from outside the canonical box at the Hebrew text of Gen 2:7. Not only does it offer a rather different view of earth's making and of our own: it does so by stressing our oneness with earth.

The Revised Standard Version translates this verse as follows:

Then the Lord God formed man of dust from the ground and breathed into his nostrils the breath of life and man became a living being.

However, in order to capture the flavor and meaning of the original text, the words *'adam* (man) and *'adamah* (dust) should be translated in ways that (a) are not gender specific and (b) that communicate the integral connection of humanity with earth. The Hebrew should therefore be rendered into English in such ways as these:

Then God Yahweh formed an *earthling* of clods from the *earth* and breathed into its nostril the breath of life; and the *earthling* became a living being. (Meyers)

Then God Yahweh formed a *human* from clods of the *humus* and breathed into its nostrils the breath of life, and the *human* became a living being. (Meyers)

IHVH Elohim fashions the *groundling*, dust of the *ground*. He blows in his nostrils the blast of life and there is the *groundling*, a living soul. (Korsak)

then Yahweh God formed the *earth creature* of dust from the *earth* and breathed into its nostrils the breath of life, and the earth creature became a living *nephesh*. (Trible)

Carol Meyers points out that to translate *'adam* as "man" is to imply a priority for male existence and also to ignore a magnificent Hebrew wordplay. The word for the stuff from which the first human being is formed is *'adamah*, usually translated as "ground" or "earth." The words for "human" and for "ground" are thus connected phonetically and perhaps etymologically. The English word "human" is not the combination of *hu* with *man*, but rather is derived from a hypothetical Indo-European root (*ghum*) meaning "earth" or "ground," from which come the Latin *humus* (earth) and the Old English *guma* (man).

She also points out that names or substantives were not simply labels; they were indicators of the very essence of the thing or creature designated. The term *'adam* suggests that the essence of human life is not to be seen in its eventual classification into gendered categories, but rather in its organic connection to the earth. And the earth in this case is not general, vague, unspecified soil or ground but rather *'adamah*, that reddish brown substance that is capable of absorbing water, being cultivated and supporting life. A friend of mine who is a Kabbalist scholar translates *'adamah* as "a mixture of blood and breath." At the very outset then, human existence is portrayed as intimately related to that which makes life possible: land, water, blood and air. It emerges *out of* the matter of which earth is constituted, the prior emergence of which is essential for our existence as air-breathing creatures.[3] This fact is reinforced today as we learn the hard way about our absolute dependence on the life-sustaining qualities of earth and air.

But even as proper translations of the Hebrew expand our vision, the notion persists that we are made up of separate parts — body and spirit — and that only the body comes out of the earth. The spirit is assumed to be inserted directly into us by God from somewhere outside this world. (This goes back to the Platonic concept of the soul "falling" into the world and materiality.) But in all the translations given, it is the fusion of earth and breath that creates life; a "living being," a *nephesh*, emerges only when earth and air, humus and spirit, come together. This is still the case.

There is no breath, no spirit without life. Nor can there be life without earth, air and water to sustain it; the hard data of science leave us in no doubt of the intimate interaction between them. Such readings of the text as those given above do not allow us to imagine, on the basis of a false asceticism, that with enough effort we can separate out the component parts of flesh and spirit in ourselves. Neither do they allow us to presume that God did not use earth as well as spirit in our making. That is to assume spirit comes from God and flesh does not, and therefore flesh "deserves" divine wrath and damnation.

Nor do we find any suggestion that the spiritual or rational element of human beings ought to control their earthliness (*'adamah)*, or that their welfare and salvation ought to take precedence over that of all other beings. In an ecological view of ourselves, the fusion of earth, blood, breath, and life makes us bodies of interacting spirit, intelligence, and matter that interrelate continuously with other such bodies — never independent of them, but radically dependent on them for our existence. We are not put on earth as subjects of a king, or as exemplars or victims of a series of behavioral laws. We are not put on earth at all. We *are* earth. Every individual being is intrinsic to the whole and plays a part in what it becomes. An ecological view of the self does not identify us primarily in terms of race, color, class, ability, sex, or occupation; rather it assigns us to the all-subsuming category of "earthling" or "groundling": an earth creature.

An ecological vision of the God presented in the Genesis text does not accord with the notion of a God external to earth and exercising transcendent divine power over it. Why not? Because the earth really is filled with the breath of God and with God's glory; and everything that lives and breathes on earth can and does praise God. When we take these words of the Psalmist to heart, the behavior of individual characters in the Genesis account takes on a rather different appearance. Whether they obey or resist an interdiction or a prescription, whether they respect or disregard a set of rules, may simply reflect all-too-normal human behavior.

The figure of Eve plays an exemplary role in this regard. The fact that for so long she has been cast in a tragic role says much about the audience's preconceptions of the plot and their expectations of her part in it. As Mary Chilton Callaway reminded us earlier, it is well-nigh impossible now to read or hear her part in the Genesis text outside the framework of salvation history. Nevertheless, we must make the attempt. I will begin with as neutral a rendering as possible of the text, a simple rehearsal of the account it presents. Then I will examine a familiar interpretation of the story, pinpointing some of the ideas such an interpretation both assumes and presents as axiomatic — even though they are not explicit in the story.

### Genesis read non-hierarchically

The story really begins for us with the first account of the creation of man and woman on the sixth day (Gen 1:24–31), when they alone out of all creation are made in the image and likeness of God. They are blessed with fertility, dominion over the earth and food from every plant and tree. It has been suggested that this first narrative arose in the context of a vegetarian, pre-hunter-gatherer society, in contrast to the social context of Genesis 9, which states that every thing that moves and lives on earth shall be food for the sons of Noah. Wherever it arose, the idyllic picture of Genesis 1, in which the culmination of God's work is the creation of Adam and Eve, serves as prologue to a second account: creation followed by decisive action (Gen 2:7–3:24).[4]

In this second account the order of creation is reversed (humans come first, then the rest of nature) and instead of a simultaneous production of male and female, man is created before woman. Some feminist readers propose on the basis of the first account (which accords superiority to the last created) that this establishes woman's superiority over man. But this, of course, is simply to fall into the hierarchical trap of assuming that someone has to be superior.

However we evaluate it, creation is described as a process, not as a *fait accompli*. God is a potter, shaping the earth creature from the dust of the earth, and the one who breathes into this earthling to animate it. God is also the gardener who plants a special garden, a "Paradise" where this creature may live in delight. There is never a hint that an earthling could live other than in this environment of plants and trees. There is never a hint, either, that God could live elsewhere.

Some of the trees are named: the tree of life and the tree of the knowledge of good and evil. The garden is watered by a river flowing out of Eden (delight) and dividing into four.[5] It is a place where waters flow continuously, in which there is no fear of drought. The trees are pleasant to see and their fruit good to eat. God permits the earthling to eat from all the trees but one. Then God gives him company: beasts and birds that the man names. But he still lacks a proper helper and companion until God puts him to sleep, removes one of his ribs, and from it fashions him a true partner. She is brought to him and named "woman." Following his approving acceptance of her, the two are declared to be united in one flesh, and sexuality thereby reunites what had been differentiated.

The events of the following scenes flow from a single decision and a single action. The serpent, introduced as the shrewdest creature in the animal world, quickly persuades the woman to eat the fruit of the forbidden tree. This dialogue, the first recorded conversation in the text, brings together on stage the animal, divine, human and plant worlds. Human life and human death are defined in terms of not-eating and eating, and the knowledge of good and evil is similarly defined.

The woman takes, eats, and gives to the man who is with her. Their eyes are opened as the serpent predicted, but they do not die as God had said. They are evicted from the garden and judgment is passed on them and *[handwritten top margin:]* If God put both trees there — one to die — one to live forever exit mentions only the one to die, God must have wanted them to eat from it

86      **Making God Laugh**

*[handwritten left margin:]* Similarity of the 2 trees in that God is working w/us — bring about meiosis each a form of death

on the serpent. The latter is cursed with a peculiar posture and food, and with perpetual enmity between its offspring and those of the woman. The woman is to suffer pain in childbirth and unsatisfied yearning for man who will rule over her. The man is not directly cursed, but sentenced to lifelong toil and sweat to obtain food from the ground upon which he has brought a curse.

Then, because the man recognized his nakedness, God makes garments and clothes the two of them, saying that now man is "like one of us, knowing good and evil. Let him not put out his hand and take from the tree of life also and eat and live for ever!"

To prevent that from occurring, God expels them both from the garden of Eden, and obliges them to serve the ground from which they were taken (Gen 3:23). After they depart, God stations the Cherubim with a flaming sword to bar them from returning to the garden and the tree of life.

We should note that the relationships between the characters and their world link the curse upon the earth caused by these humans with the curse upon the serpent. It must eat dust from the earth all the days of its life. They must eat of the earth in pain and toil until they return to the dust eaten by the serpent, the same dust from which they themselves were formed. The outcome of the action focuses on the judgments that result from the woman's dealings with the serpent. The good earth is cursed; plants give way to thorns and thistles; fulfilling work has become alienating labor; power over animals has deteriorated into enmity with their representative, the serpent; sexuality (for woman) has splintered into unfulfilled longing and subordination. The fruit that is eaten has become a symbol of the knowledge of good and evil. The fruit that is not eaten is the ability to live forever. In the dialogue between the woman and the serpent, the man stands silently by and God is offstage. God appears only after they have acted, to question and pass judgment on their actions. Only then does the man speak; he calls the woman Eve, "because she is the mother of all the living."

### Common perceptions of the Genesis story

Now we may focus on the blanket presupposition – summed up in the Book of Common Prayer as "the condition of man after the fall of Adam" – that usually colors our perception of what happens in the story. While the interconnectedness of relationships between God, humankind and the plant and animal world is taken for granted, it is usually assumed that as the result of human actions they have changed for the worse. Hence the story is perceived as a tragedy, in which the kind of interconnectedness between woman, man, and Nature established and desired by God is shattered for all of them.

Further, the story has been received as an account of origins, told from the point of view of a witness who recorded the events more or less accurately as they occurred. The effect, then, is to take us from a beginning in nothingness or chaos through the delights of Eden on to the denouement of a shattered world. The Creator remains the same throughout, directing events before the decisive action by Eve as well as after it. Reading the story as an account of origins has had the effect of treating the characters and actions as prototypes, not archetypes. To grasp the difference, we must appreciate that the characters present the *essential* (archetypal) features of human life at the time the story was recorded. But that does not make them the *first* (prototypical) humans in a historical sense. The depicted features of their life are those thought by the story-teller to be shared by all humanity.[6] The Church Fathers' classification of the characters and their actions as prototypes (first man and woman, first parents, first sin), has reinforced a linear concept of time that leads some Christians to assume that this is a story of origins that faithfully chronicles the origins of life on earth.

But who could this chronicler be who sees everything "in the beginning?" Who but God was there when the heavens and the earth were created? The acceptance of God in the role of chronicler masks three further assumptions about the story itself. First, that God intended human beings to live for ever and in a state of perfect harmony with the more-than-human world and its creator. Second, that the characters known as Adam and Eve disregarded God's intentions and wrecked the divine plan thus bringing death into the world. And finally, that therefore the original plan had to be revised by God – a revision elaborated and preached by Church Fathers such as Augustine.

An outstanding characteristic of all these assumptions is the supremely arrogant one that biblical and patristic authors can speak authoritatively for God. This in turn presupposes that human words can fully or even adequately express divine purposes. A glance back at chapter one and the discussion there of "learnéd ignorance" should quickly disabuse us of the notion that language can ever fully express truth; above all that it can encompass the truth of the absolute mystery we call God.

Another imported assumption about the Genesis story is one mentioned already: that this is a story of sin, of Adam's "fall" through Eve's initiative. Her punishment, to bear children in pain, is judged as a more severe punishment than man's struggles with the soil. Therefore her sin is assumed to be greater than man's. Her desire for her husband is seen as God's way of keeping her subordinate and submissive to him. God has ordained that man should have control over woman and over an earth cursed because of his disobedience.

God's actions and words are read through a hierarchical grid in some of the following ways. He is male. And he creates man first. Both of these features of the story are taken to mean that man is superior to woman. God punishes them both because they reject his authority to tell them what to do and what not to do — and ultimately his power over their life and death. In such a theocracy, God exercises this power not only over them, but over the plants and animals as well, and therefore can decide to punish them too — not for anything they have done, but for the misbehavior of the woman and man. Even though the earth has played no part in their actions, and the serpent only an indirect one, the former is cursed because of man and the serpent's issue placed under the woman's heel. They are to live under human control, a control delegated by God to man in a theocratic world.

Because God is said to have placed the man and woman in a garden of delights, one must presume it was his intention for them to stay there. But his will for them also required a certain course of action that they refused to follow. His will ranks above his desire for their happiness, and his will has been disobeyed. Even though God wanted them to be happy, even more did he desire their obedience. Our relationship with God is then defined as one of submission to divine will, in effect submission shown to those to whom divine power has supposedly been delegated — or who have arrogated such power to themselves in God's name.

God, it is agreed, did not want humanity to suffer. So he placed the man and woman in Eden, a setting that by its very name precludes the notion of suffering. Having disobeyed, they were banished from the delights of Paradise. It was their fault. If we do not obey God, then we too suffer, and what we endure is *our* own fault. Moreover, universal suffering is inevitable, since through Eve's disobedience, women must suffer the pain of bearing men's seed while filled with unsatisfied yearning for its possessor; the animal world is locked in enmity with that seed and must bear the pain of subjection to it; and men must toil and suffer to scratch out a livelihood from the soil that is cursed through association with them.

Furthermore, the inclination to disobey and its consequence, pain, are now part of our nature because our will to obey has been disordered by our ancestors' refusal to obey God's order. We continue to disobey and therefore know for ourselves what it is to suffer God's judgments. If we accept suffering properly, that is, acknowledge it to be punishment for sin and a result of our flawed character, then God may readmit us to Paradise after our death.

### The rise and growth of these perceptions

Many if not all of these interpretations were current before and during the fourth century of the Common Era – the time when Augustine wrote and preached on the Genesis narrative – though as we shall see, his ideas did not go unchallenged. He inherited perceptions from the patriarchal cultures of Greece and the Roman Empire and from the Hebrew worldview appropriated by the Christian tradition and handed on through the writing and preaching of Church Fathers and bishops. We find, for example, such Second Testament passages as 1 Tim 2:13–14: "For Adam was formed first, then Eve; and Adam was not deceived, but the woman was deceived and became a transgressor." By the early centuries of the Christian era, this and similar attitudes toward Eve were commonplace in religious literature. The association of Eve with temptation, sexuality, and lust proliferated in both Christian and Jewish post-biblical sources, with the serpent playing an increasingly satanic and phallic role. And of course the more Eve is identified as the source of sin, the more urgent becomes the need to control, subdue and dominate her.

The negative thrust of these interpretations was exacerbated by translations of the Hebrew which subtly changed and distorted the meaning. The patriarchal views of Jerome, for example, colored his extremely influential translation of the Hebrew Scriptures into Latin. Note, for example, how the version used by Augustine renders Genesis 3:16, the passage in which God addresses Eve after she and Adam have eaten the forbidden fruit:

> I will multiply your toils and your conceptions; in grief you will
> bear children, and you will be under the power of your husband,
> and he will rule over you.

By interpreting "rule" as being "under the power of your husband," Jerome introduces an absolutism lacking in the Hebrew original. This notion of power over a woman's body resonated with certain strands in the Christian tradition received by Jerome. In the writings and life of Cyprian of Carthage we get the picture of an embattled male community, the "tight bond of brotherhood" of the Christian church drawn up in battle array against the secular world of Roman society behind whose brutality Cyprian sensed the abiding presence of the devil and his angels. Christians were "in the fighting line" of the devil's war against the human race. With decisive effect Cyprian bequeathed to Ambrose, Jerome, and Augustine a view of the human body influenced by this overriding preoccupation. The flesh of the Christian was a bulwark against the world. It might be dedicated to Christ in virginity by men and women in order to preserve its integrity, but it remained in perpetual danger as an outpost of the self tensed to receive the myriad blows of the world. The body of the Christian was a microcosm of the threatened state of the church, which itself was a compact body, held in firm restraint by the unshakeable God-given will of its head and guiding mind, the bishop.

Ambrose was just such a bishop, and Augustine another. For Ambrose, human sexual feeling stood in dark contrast to the blaze of Christ's untouched body. But by conversion and baptism in the Catholic Church, the one body was transformed into the other, and human bodies "scarred" by sexuality could be redeemed by a body whose virgin birth had rendered it exempt from sexual desire. Indeed, baptism was an intimate participation in this perfect flesh of Christ. Such a contrast between the birth of Christ and the birth of ordinary human beings would provide Augustine with what he took to be irrefutable support of his own views on the causative relation between the act of intercourse and the transmission of "original sin."[7]

Having become standard terminology for much of Christian spirituality, these themes of a battle to retain power over the world, sexuality, and flesh had another outlet once Constantine adopted the Cross as a symbol of victory in the battles of the Roman Empire. The marching columns of the imperial army became a model of the Christian battle against the pagan world so vividly portrayed by Cyprian. Violence in the name of the perfect flesh of Christ against the flesh of the unbaptized and the pagan was sanctified. Before Cyprian, Tertullian had made the momentous choice to employ the word *sacramentum* – a term for a Roman soldier's oath of allegiance to the Emperor – for the baptismal vow. Military metaphors still abound today in baptismal services and in hymns associated with incorporation into the body of Christ.

It is crucial for us to recognize that Augustine's soon-to-be-standard interpretation of the creation account arose within the context of a hierarchical Roman society in which Emperors commanded their subjects to live or die in a particular manner. Landowners exploited and flogged peasants who toiled on their lands. Male heads of households exercised absolute authority over wives, children, and slaves. Augustine so concurred with these prescriptive agencies that in 405 CE he agreed to the use of Roman power to forcibly "reunite" Donatist congregations with the Catholic Church. That is, the hierarchical structures of secular authority that gave cohesion to society might properly be called upon to support the Catholic Church.[8]

This link between Christianity and physical violence, whether forged for the benefit of ecclesiastical expansion or spiritual purity, is one of the ugliest manifestations of the church's hierarchical character and its perception of power. It has sanctioned military, domestic, and economic violence of the cruelest kind. Rape and pillage are the inseparable companions of war, and religious wars have been no exception.[9] In a foreshadowing of contemporary ecofeminist concerns, the witch trials and burnings carried out by Christian authorities in both Europe and America were sanctioned on the grounds that woman's dark side, her lust and wanton sexuality, were associated with unruly Nature. The blame for the bodily corruption of the male was attributed directly to temptation by the female after the example of Eve. The supposed disorder wrought by lusty women was portrayed in hundreds of paintings and graphics on witchcraft produced from the end of the fifteenth century until the close of the seventeenth.

These, together with the Dominican tract that articulated church doctrine against witches (the *Malleus Maleficarum*, popularly known as "The Hammer of Witches"), were the basis of the witch trials. This tract stated that woman conspires constantly against spiritual good, because of her insatiable natural lust, and therefore she consorts with devils and is especially prone to the crime of witchcraft, from which men have been preserved by the maleness of Christ.[10] Not only were women the majority of the accused (some authorities give figures of a hundred to one), but they came primarily from the lowest social orders and were largely illiterate. Clearly, religious, social, and sexual attitudes towards women and Nature played a significant part in delineating the victims.

I want to draw additional attention here to a point I made in the opening chapter. The repeated use of battle imagery to model both the individual Christian's relationship with his or her body and by extension, with the body of Christ, together with its external manifestation in religious wars and the persecution of witches, inevitably linked the notion of divine power to the image of government by force. Relationship to divinity became defined in terms of the dynamics of hierarchical relationships of power, in which one exerted power and repressive control over one's own body, or a group of men with physical and spiritual power exerted it over individuals or other groups. In either case it was, of course, all done in the name of God. Those under control were taught to see salvation in terms of absolute submission to this power.[11]

Luther's major commentary on Genesis, which incorporated earlier interpretations, was written when Emperors and Electors controlled armies, fathers had absolute authority in households, and husbands' absolute control over wives. He rebuked his own son's disobedience on the grounds that it was offensive to God's majesty. He also witnessed the horror of a widespread peasants' revolt, the savage suppression of which by an alliance of princes and bishops he initially endorsed. On the day when Bishop Conrad rode in triumph into Würzburg, the event was celebrated with the execution of sixty-four burghers and peasants, after which the bishop — accompanied by the executioner — made a tour of his diocese.

This revolt and others — like that in Britain in 1369 put down by "martial bishop" Henry Despenser — broke out when peasants were unable to meet their overlords' demands for rents or taxes. If their crop failed or their taxes rose, they might well see their families starve and their holdings seized. Of course, the Augustinian hypothesis that such hardships were both the result and punishment of sin reflected assumptions that arose in part from the enigmatic character of suffering in everyday experience. The theory became self-reinforcing because the "explanation" of the world's ills also functioned as the sanction for the repressive present order. It further served to stifle dissatisfaction because it both answered people's questions about the perennial inequities of the natural and social worlds and provided justification for those answers.

When it came, then, to interpreting the Genesis narrative, there were no competing images to place against that of God as a despotic parent who demanded under pain of death total obedience from the creatures of a world under his power. Nor was it a cause for wonder that such a God should be presumed to have punished this sinful flouting of his will by suffering inflicted on those who had sinned and all their descendants. The flaming sword set against Adam and Eve was a powerful reminder of the weapons that bishops raised against the declared enemies of church and state.

## Wider implications

The wider implications of such hierarchical relationships, especially the suffering, willfulness, and violence which pervaded them, were the catastrophe which Augustine set out to explain. He did so systematically by seeing the present state of affairs, in which cruelty and coercion were built into the structures of society, as evidence of the distortion of the human will through Adam's "fall." The original God-given bonds of control in human society — friendship, marriage, and paternal command — had given way under the endless assaults of willfulness that strained those bonds, broke them, and ultimately changed their nature. Adam and Eve, he surmised, had originally enjoyed a harmonious unity of body and soul which no longer existed on any level.

For this reason, death remained for Augustine the bitterest sign of human frailty. For death frustrated the soul's deepest wish, which was to live at peace with its beloved, the body. Death was now an "unnatural" occurrence. He connected this with the disjunction between conscious will and sexual feeling which seemed to betray a dislocation of the human person quite as appalling as was the obscene anomaly of death. Indeed, for Augustine sexual intercourse was the very epitome of death. Like death, the onset and culmination of sexual sensation mocked the will. Its random movements spoke of a primal dislocation, an abiding principle of discord lodged in the human person since "the fall." It had not been so, he conjectured, in Paradise, where will and sexual delight had run together in perfect accord for Adam and Eve. Any married intercourse before the fall would have been an object lesson in the balanced rapture with which all human beings might have used the physical joys showered upon them by their Creator. Only in the virgin birth of Christ, he declared, had Mary recaptured Eve's first potential bodily harmony.

This had important psychological and physiological implications, for sexuality was effectively removed from its physiological context and made to mirror an abiding, unhealed fissure in the soul. For Augustine, the uncontrollable elements in sexual desire revealed the existence of a permanent spiritual flaw that inclined the human person irrevocably towards the flesh. But this flesh was not simply the body: it was the whole complex of venal desires that led the self to prefer its own will to that of God. With Adam's fall, the soul lost the ability to summon itself in an undivided act of will to love and praise God in all created things. This incapacity was the sign of a human race condemned by God's justice to endure the reciprocal punishment of a body and a soul both wracked by the unalterable consequences of mankind's first sin. Peter Brown recaptures Augustine's vision thus:

> Only by baptism and by incorporation into the Catholic Church, a church whose basilicas were now plainly visible in every city of the Roman world, and whose hierarchy embraced and disciplined all forms of Christian life, would human beings be enabled to join the one city of which *glorious things* might be spoken: the Heavenly Jerusalem, the City of God. Only in a city at the end of time, and in no city of the Western Empire in its last century, would the ache of discord, so faithfully mirrored in the flesh by sexuality, give way to a *pax plena*, to a fullness of peace.[12]

It is hardly surprising that this powerful systematic exposition by Augustine of the connection between the Genesis narrative and the world of his day, in conjunction with concepts derived from the image of God as King and Maker, should have had powerful and enduring effects on Christianity. The cruelty and coercion evident in relationships between human beings and between them and Nature was explained by their condemnation to this state through the justice of God on account of sin. Christian notions of human creation, death, and sexuality tended to wrench the human person loose from the physical world. Rather than seeing humanity as systemically linked with the fertility of Nature and dependent on natural elements, the individual person was seen in relation to a distortion of the human will, a radical disharmony between what God intended us to be and what we are. Paradoxically, perhaps, Augustine saw the restoration of that harmony in social terms, as the eventual redemption of human society.

By seemingly detaching us from Nature other than as necessary for the sustenance of life, we came to see it as something external to ourselves to be controlled by human will. But this assumption of the right to control was established by presupposing the primacy of spirit and will over the body. The indissoluble connection between sexuality, sin, and female fertility served only to strengthen the determination to master both woman and Nature. Indeed, people were discouraged from participating in the pleasures appropriate to their animal nature and thereby realizing their rootedness in the things of earth; rather they were urged to aspire to the glorious things of heaven. Human prayer to the one God, offered by those who strove to control the flesh by the will, replaced the natural cosmic praise which linked the exuberant earth with the transcendent God.

Sermons in church buildings kept alight the great hope of future transformation at the end of time, when Paradise would be regained. Far from guaranteeing salvation, the human condition jeopardized it. By an increasing and finally total insistence that its hierarchy adopt celibacy, a way of life uncontaminated by sexuality, the Catholic Church made plain that it enjoyed a supernatural guarantee of patriarchal continuity based on baptism administered by men who did not themselves beget children. The genetic covenant with Abraham was replaced with the umbilical cord of apostolic succession.[13]

These historic phenomena created a climate in which control over Nature was taken for granted. The development of baptism into a form of re-birth that eschewed natural birth denied any creature born through biological processes alone its inherent relationship with the divine. All creatures other than baptized human beings were relegated to a profane, unsacred, and irreverenced status. The results of this dualism have been devastating.

In the context of this chapter, where we have been looking at hierarchies functioning as theocracies of divine power over creation, it is possible to affirm a gradual though not widespread improvement in the regard accorded to women today. Now that the secular world has recognized the inherent injustice of sexism, it cannot publicly be claimed as a mark of the true church. But insofar as ecclesiastical hierarchies were and are structures that arrogate to human males a special relationship with divinity, and only through them to women, sexism in the name of God still holds sway in the churches. Jerome's translation of Genesis is still part of the Christian rationale for the exercise of power over women. Moreover, Christian hierarchical presuppositions about our relationship with Nature remain unchanged. Earth, personified as Nature, is still perceived as existing *by divine decree* solely for the sake of humankind. In a culture that envisions mastery as the realm of men, the male self comes to be identified with all that represents control, spirit, and transcendence of Nature. This skewed perception is in direct contrast to contemporary ecological consciousness of the connectedness between humanity and earth, between *humus* and the human person.

# 8

# Changing Perceptions of Genesis

I n dealing with the Genesis text, an even closer look within the box reveals that several canonized Christian words and concepts central to the Augustinian hypothesis of "original sin" simply do not occur there. For instance, we find no apple – even though the figure of a woman holding one has consistently identified Eve in the popular mind. For example, a modern staging of a mediaeval play – in which Christ descends into hell to tell the souls there that they have been redeemed from sin through his death – makes Eve instantly identifiable by a large glossily painted wooden apple in her hand. It would be difficult to identify Adam were it not that he clasps Eve's other hand.

The supposed reason for what the third Article of the Book of Common Prayer calls "the going down of Christ into Hell" (and indeed, for the existence of Hell and its considerable population) is "the condition of man after the fall of Adam." Yet the Genesis text contains neither the word nor the idea of a fall. This concept has been so hard-programmed into Christianity that it is assumed to derive from the text itself. In fact, the association of a fall with the creation of humanity comes from the *Phaedrus*, in which Plato describes heavenly perfections shedding their wings and *falling* to earth to be implanted and born as humans. The application of this image to the Genesis text radically distorts the meaning of the Hebrew original of God fashioning from the earth two creatures who become living souls. It is also misleading in regard to the Platonic text because there the "fall" is integral to the creation of human beings and unrelated to their subsequent actions.

It must be conceded that Christian interpreters did not use Platonic imagery in order to mislead, but to show the goodness of what God did in creating us; their aim was to safeguard the belief that everything a good God did or does is good. In the Platonic tradition, the ideal form of unity – the idea of the One that has long occupied an exalted place in the world of ideas – is a unity without parts, a unity without differentiation or division of any kind. It is a unity of this absolute sort that the Church Fathers claimed to be characteristic of God. According to Irenaeus, "God is simple uncompounded being"; "No parts are to be ascribed to God, for the One is indivisible," says Clement of Alexandria; and Origen concurs: "God is one and altogether simple."[1]

### Common perceptions of Genesis 1–3

Faced with the ungodly reality of suffering, cruelty, and willfulness, Christian interpreters took the Platonic notion of creation as fall and applied it to the *actions* of those first created. Casting Adam and Eve as prototypes meant that their actions could be seen to affect all subsequent creation of human life through human procreation. Human birth, Augustine could then argue, was the result of a sexual act that was essentially flawed because it was not under the perfect control of the will. And the will itself was "fallen"; that is, it was not in control because it had been irrevocably damaged by the willful disobedience of the first (prototypical) woman and man. (As I shall point out in chapter eleven, this foreshadows our contemporary understanding of genetic inheritance.)

Furthermore, this modified concept of fall applied to the Genesis story is inextricably bound to yet other concepts – those of *sin* and *redemption*. And yet, just as the word "fall" is not in the text, the word "sin" appears nowhere in the first three chapters of Genesis. Even though the account is commonly read as a narrative about the beginnings of sin in the world, none of the Hebrew words for sin and transgression are used in these chapters. When God pronounces judgment on the specific act which leads to the couple's eviction from the garden, only the act itself is given as the reason. Interpreters may stress the breach of God's will this act entails, and exegetes may study it in the context of other passages about sin; but the text includes no such label, nor does it make or attribute to God any such connection. Nor does the Hebrew Bible ever associate any of the many sins later committed by the children of Israel with this behavior in the garden. Even the prophets, who continually harangue the Israelites about their sinful behavior, never mention Adam and Eve. In their thoroughly detailed indictments and warnings about sin, judgment, punishment, and banishment, the prophets "threw the book" at erring kings and idolatrous peoples – but they never mentioned its first three chapters.[2]

*Human choice and the discrimination of good + evil: what I say the border is about*

The word "sin" first appears in the Hebrew Scriptures in Genesis 4. There, just before the murder of Abel, God warns Cain that "sin is crouching at the door." According to the Christian biblical scholar Gottfried Quell, the masculine Hebrew noun used for "sin" (*hatta'th*) represents a demonic being, and the intended image is God calling Cain's attention to this figure who is waiting for him to choose between doing the right thing and the wrong thing – a choice that will either deliver him from sin or ensnare him in its grasp.[3]

Yet commenting on the narrative in Genesis 3, Quell states that its author shows "with absolutely convincing simplicity, which a child could understand, how sin happens, what it is, and what it leads to." He then points out how remarkable it is that the usual technical Hebrew concepts for sin, all of which he has enumerated, are all lacking in this text! His next sentence reads, "The reader is only aware that this is a story about sin." Not content with that bald assertion, he quarrels in a footnote with another scholar who argues that this view originated – centuries later – with the Deuteronomists. Contradicting this, Quell states categorically, "The Israelite author [of Genesis 3] knew, as well as all his readers, that sin is the main point of the story." Did God know, I wonder?[4]

Quell's assertion is hardly surprising. The English translation of his work on sin in the Hebrew Bible opens with a quotation from William Law: "The whole nature of the Christian religion stands on these two great pillars, namely, the greatness of our fall and the greatness of our redemption." Reading the Genesis text within this canonical structure, people may indeed think they have correctly understood its main point. But if it was so evident to the author, why didn't he say so as clearly as he does in the very next chapter by painting a vivid picture of God warning Cain of sin? May it not simply be the case that at any point in history murder is clearly a sin but eating a piece of fruit from a tree is not? Or are we being asked to believe in a God who considers them equally grave? *What clearly is*

The author of Genesis also fails to make two other connections obvious to traditional Christian scholars. Nowhere is Cain's horrendous deed linked with his parents' act of disobedience, nor are the events in Eden related to any subsequent sins or to the human proclivity for sin.

This brings us to yet another curious fact. Apart from these early chapters of Genesis, the Hebrew Bible contains no further mention of Eve, the figure who in later Christian interpretations carries the symbolic apple identifying her as the prototypical sinner. She reappears (though not by name) in the deuterocanonical book called Ben Sira after the Jewish sage who wrote it. Written in Hebrew and translated into Greek in the second century BCE, this book appears in the Roman Catholic canon as *Ecclesiasticus*, but was omitted from the Hebrew and Protestant canons. Alluding to Eve, the author says, "From a woman was the beginning of sin, and because of her we all died." (Sir 24:25)

In associating a woman with the origins of sin, Ben Sira was in a minority. His contemporaries tended to ascribe it to Adam or, on the basis of Genesis 6:1–4, to the fall of evil angels and their cohabitation with women. Nevertheless, as the first known author to state that sin and death are the negative results of a woman's act, this early sage provided one of the most extraordinarily tenacious interpretations of the Genesis narrative. Its persistence, as we saw in the previous chapter, had much to do with its systematic elaboration by Christian exegetes living in patriarchal cultures before and after Augustine, most obviously its reiteration in such passages as 1 Timothy 2:13–14.

### Interpretations based on uncanonical perceptions

Once out of the shadow of the canonical pillars of "fall and redemption", we are able to read the dialogues in Genesis with new eyes. We find for example that God simply told the earthlings the consequence of eating the fruit: if they did, they would die. The serpent denies that, and tells them of another consequence: they will become like God, knowing good from evil. The woman sees that the fruit is good to eat, "to get insight from," and she takes it and eats. She gives it to the man and he does the same. Their eyes are opened and they do not die.

God tells them the potential results of their action, but the decision is theirs. God does not say: "If you do one or the other, you are behaving in a good way or a bad way," or "You will please or displease me." God simply says, "You will die." The serpent says, "You will become like God, knowing good and evil." Both describe consequences, not – as has been long inferred – divine preferences. If certain actions are taken, certain consequences follow. It is also worth noting that the serpent's prediction soon comes true, while God's is, against expectation, not immediately effective. The woman and man do not die upon eating the fruit. Having learned the difference between good and evil, they live on and eventually die in conditions recognizable to any ancient Palestinian. Rather more significant is that on being expelled from Eden, they recognize that to survive they must serve the earth from which they were taken.[5]

The Christian tradition has generally assumed that not eating that particular fruit – that is remaining unaware of right and wrong – is good. This would lead one to the inescapable conclusion that God did not want them *addition to Response to Sermons 3+4* [handwritten]

to know good from evil. But this idea stands in stark contrast to another well-known story in the Hebrew Scriptures. When Solomon had consolidated his rule over Israel, the Lord appeared to him in a dream and asked him what he wanted. Solomon replied – or so the author tells us – that because God had made him king in place of his father David and given him a great multitude of people to govern, he desired above all an understanding mind, "that I may discern between good and evil" (1 Kings 3:9).

God is pleased that Solomon asked for this rather than for "long life or riches or the life of your enemies" – indeed so pleased that he grants the new king these as well! It should also be noted that the same Ben Sira who charges woman with bringing sin and death into the world personifies Wisdom as a female who cries out to Israel: "Come to me, you who desire me, and eat your fill of my fruit!" (Sir 24:19).

In the Genesis narrative it is Eve who, in dialogue with the wisest of the animals, the serpent (Matt 10:16), perceives the desirability of gaining understanding of good and evil. Elizabeth Cady Stanton took this dialogue to show that the serpent found in the woman that intense thirst for knowledge that the simple pleasures of picking flowers and talking with Adam did not satisfy. Shaw's black girl would applaud this reading. And although Augustine's God would not be one to enjoy the joke, her God certainly would.

Close attention to the text should make us wary of the assumption that God did not want the woman and man to know good from evil. What a very infantile and hapless pair they would have remained! For that matter, how could Eve have "sinned" in taking the apple before she had eaten it and so come to know right from wrong? What about exegetes who read the story and presume themselves capable to make judgments about the goodness or evil of the actions recorded there and to label some of them "sin"? Would they consider themselves fully human without these moral faculties? Would they forego them in order to keep God happy? Do they believe God would deprive us of that knowledge in order to protect his divinity? *[handwritten: Yes!]*

Even if we ignore some of these logical consequences, taking the outcome of actions as intimations of whether or not they were desired by God, Ben Sira leaves us with a further discrepancy based on the cause-and-effect relationship between sin and punishment presumed to govern the Genesis story. His blunt statement that sin and death came into the world through woman overlooks the important fact that the woman is named Eve only *after* she has taken the fruit and eaten it. Her name, literally translated in the text itself lest its significance be lost, means "the mother of all the living." How, then, can Ben Sira make her the mother of death? *[handwritten: argument to John, re #20]*

*Idea for my death: Have family members make a coffin for my body, and have all my family members write something or draw pictures on the coffin & covering it with whatever feelings they have about me — ourselves — ourselves. The day it — not sure how until cremation*

Yet that connection between sin, death, and woman has become so much part of Christian consciousness as to lead to the assumption that God wanted Eve neither to sin nor to die. It was her own fault that she did both. This leads to the further assumption that God never intended us to die either.[6]

*maybe do this as a whole. as I brief a draw*

*for — attend you when you were born, surrounding you with thoughts, feelings, memories, & much else — especially love — please do the same for me in my death.*

### Augustine and Julian of Eclanum

*and/or put a symbol of some kind inside the casket with me — if someone has unfinished business will write me a note + put it/them in the coffin — photographs included too! flowers*

This assumption was made in masterly fashion by Augustine, who used it to create a conceptual bridge between the pillars of "fall and redemption." It was hotly contested in Augustine's lifetime by Julian of Eclanum. He held the view that mortality is not the result of sin but of nature. Why, he asked, does Genesis not say that *because Adam sinned* he would return to dust? His return to the earth is not linked to sin. Instead, Julian argues, the author says that because he came from the earth, he would return to it. Because of our nature, our intrinsic connection with the systemic creature earth, we die and our bodies disintegrate back into their organic elements.

Also, Julian argued, God created and blessed human fertility even before Eve's taking the fruit (Gen 1:28). In the normal course of events, human beings were to replenish their numbers on earth depleted by mortality. The command to increase and fill the earth supposes that there will be room for that increase; but if everyone were to survive, then the earth would soon become not simply filled, but overwhelmed.

*have Melanie (British painting the casket) beautiful after everyone has finished writing on it.*

This fourth century criticism of Augustine is very pertinent to our modern attitudes to death. Not only do we tend to ignore or seek to evade the consequences of increasing life-expectancy in terms of overtaxing the earth's resources: the reluctance to accept death as part of our nature lies behind the marketing of many medical advances that assume we have the right to prolong human life indefinitely.

For more than twelve years Augustine and Julian debated about human nature, sexual desire, and death. After considerable controversy, the church of the fifth century accepted Augustine's views and rejected Julian's as heretical.[7] Of great interest here are the connections Augustine made (and Julian rejected) between the centrality of human sin and its consequent effects on the more-than-human world.

Augustine argued that as a result of "original sin", not only humanity but the natural world as well became subject to death and disorder. Julian insisted that God created fully innocent natures, capable of virtue according to their will, not only in Paradise but here on Earth as well. Human nature – mortal, sexual, and vulnerable as it is – participates in the wholeness and goodness of the original creation. Augustine assumed that frustrated desire is universal, infinite and all-consuming. Julian held that sexual desire is innocent, divinely blessed, and once satisfied, entirely finite. It offers us the opportunity to exercise our capacity for moral choice. (That he himself was happily married is not surprising.) Augustine concludes that we are as help-less in the face of death as we are defenseless against sexual passion, because we are punished by death for sin. (He became a celibate after illicit and guilt-provoking experience of sexual pleasure.) Julian says this is to confuse physiology with morality. Death is not a punishment for sin but a natural process, like sexual arousal and childbirth – natural, necessary, and univer-sal for all living species. It is *spiritual* death that is a matter of choice.

This clash between two world views 1600 years ago resounds again today between those who maintain an ecological outlook and those who see hierarchy everywhere. Julian in effect pre-empted the Copernican revo-lution that the ecological vision seeks to complete; for him, humankind in the person of Adam is not the centre around which the whole of creation revolves. That we all suffer, die, inflict suffering, and make wrong moral choices does not mean that one man's actions flawed our natures irrevoca-bly. Even less does it mean that the whole structure of the universe was thereby transformed for the worse. Instead of making Adam the pivot on which the balance of the world depends, we must dislodge him (and human-ity) from that role and place ourselves within the more-than-human life-world. That way, he is but an archetypal member of one species among many others. Just as women's consciousness has alerted us to the dangers of elevating the generic male in Adam above the rest of humanity, ecological humility helps counteract the impulse to elevate the human above all other species.

Yet the canonized interpretation of the Genesis text still keeps Christianity confined in the conceptual trap of a traditional fall and sin the-ology. In spite of textual, moral, or ecological difficulties, that doctrinal stance has long stood and is still authoritatively upheld as the only true and valid account of why and how we relate to each other, to the world, and to God. The rehabilitation of Julian as an orthodox theologian is not, as far as I know, on the official Christian theological agenda, though his views con-tinue to fuel academic debate. I became a follower of his the day I realized that the beautiful little baby girl being baptized in our church was first going to be exorcized of a demon that had supposedly possessed her since the moment of birth. Or was it at conception she supposedly became "enslaved to Satan"?

If questioned, such rituals are explained by an Augustinian interpreta-tion in which God is presented as a stern and unyielding parent; Adam and

Eve appear as feckless and disobedient children as well as the ancestors
whose sin handed us over to the power of Satan; and we are radically flawed
creatures who can only be exhorted not to repeat their mistake. Any attempt
to question the thinking behind such practices is ultimately treated as
Julian's was: as a rebellion against the hierarchical authority we are told is
placed over us by God and from which comes the only remedy we have
against the flawed nature of our own judgment. In this way Augustinian
assumptions and self-perceptions are endlessly recycled until the "catch 22"
is complete. Rebellion against them is the symptom that proves the illness.
It is the same argument that Luther used against women as a warning against
any complaint of theirs about their subordination to men.

Few, I suspect, would ever dream of taking the Genesis stories second-
hand from Augustine. Fewer still would be content to overlook such textual
errors in his exegesis as his mistranslation of Romans 5:12; for here he renders, "death spread to all men because of (Adam) *in whom* all sinned" rather
than "*in that* [i. e. because] all sinned." Yet most accept without question his
fundamental assumption that human nature and this world as we now experience it are totally other than what God intended them to be. According to
this view, we were not intended to know good from evil, to be capable of
sin, to suffer, or to die. The fact that we do do all these things (which God
supposedly never intended and we find abhorrent) is explained on the
grounds of a flawed human decision by our "first" parents to eat an "apple"
expressly forbidden to them. In other words, we (humans) thwarted God's
(divine) plans for us. Surely this convoluted hypothesis exemplifies one of
the gravest of sins – that of theological presumption.

We saw these assumptions at work earlier in the discussion of the
Hebrew vocabulary for the concept of sin. And even Phyllis Trible, a recognized scholar who has done much valuable work on the Hebrew text, concludes her exegesis of the story by proposing that

> Life has lost to Death, harmony to hostility, unity and fulfilment
> to fragmentation and dispersion. The divine, human, animal and
> plant worlds are all adversely affected. Indeed, the image of God
> male and female has participated in a tragedy of disobedience.
> Estranged from each other, the man and the woman are banished
> from the garden and barred forever from the tree of life. Truly, a
> love story has gone awry.[8]

The situation is summed up perceptively by Elaine Pagels, who remarks
that if any of us could come to our own culture as a foreign anthropologist
and examine traditional Christian convictions about sexuality, and our cur-

rent view of human nature in relation to politics, philosophy, and psychology, we might well be astonished at many of the attitudes we take for granted, many of them derived from the story of Adam and Eve. Even non-Christians and Christians who see the story only as literature live in a culture indelibly shaped by interpretations of it. James Hillman insightfully remarks that the psychological history of the male-female relationship in our civilization may be seen as a series of footnotes to the tale of Adam and Eve.[9]

### Can common perceptions be changed?

The traditional interpretations analyzed in this chapter are based on the premise that sin is the paramount interpretive category for this story. If one accepts that assumption, then attitudes to women, men, and Nature that can clearly be seen as unacceptable ecologically will no doubt persist. After all, the interpretation and its conclusions have prevailed for over two millennia. Is it possible to change them now?

Before we can begin to answer that question, we have to ask why no significant change has yet taken place. One answer is implicit in the process of canonizing the tradition. As their control grew, the Church Fathers' images and arguments came to constitute the authorized Christian conceptualization of the ultimate reality of God. Their images came from the Graeco-Roman world to which they belonged and to which they were concerned to speak. The pioneering days of Greek philosophy were over, but the influence of its great schools continued in the general intellectual climate of early Christianity. Maurice Wiles sums up the situation neatly:

> The Fathers were the scholars of the Church, and both halves of the definition are important. They were scholars, seeking to express the faith in as intelligent and coherent a form as they could devise. But they were not working in a vacuum, nor in the setting of a modern secular institution. They were scholars of the Church, continually in touch with the day-to-day worshipping life of the Church.[10]

Their scholarly authority was invoked against individuals until the intellectual ferment that had characterized the great theological debates of the early centuries of the church (such as that between Augustine and Julian) was resolved into received dogma.

It was a lengthy and complex process by which Graeco-Roman concepts and imagery were filtered through an Augustinian interpretation and became absorbed into theology and church life (baptismal ceremonies and creeds, for example). This is not to put forward a conspiracy theory of Christian doctrine taken over by Greek and Latin scholars, but simply an acknowledgement of their internally coherent attempt to express the ultimate reality of God in ways that were intelligible to their contemporaries. Every such achievement is necessarily time-bound and culture-specific.

What gave theirs an enduring power was that they were, as Wiles mentioned, *Fathers* – male heirs to the divinely sanctioned authority of Christ *in the Church*. Their works were studied by generations of preachers and pastors, and became part of devotional readings in the daily Office of monks and clerics. As the generations passed and the thought-world of the Fathers grew increasingly remote, more and more time was spent on recapturing it by amplifying and qualifying their images and concepts. Theology gradually took these over as its own language and proper study, and such concepts as "incarnation", "trinity", "redemption", "fall", and "original sin" became standard terms and subjects, accepted ways of summing up the mystery of our interaction with God, with each other, and with the world.

The question that arises for the church today is whether these terms and syntheses are relevant or appropriate within the current ecological context. Do they help Christians to find meaning in their lives and work? If we employ "original sin" as an interpretive concept for our relationship with creation, do we not come to perceive the very worst side of human life as inescapable, rather than seek grounds for hope in our natural relationship with it? In a post-Darwinian world does it make sense to make man an exception to evolutionary processes?

Another important point is implicit in Wiles' statement: the church has never recognized any Church *Mothers*. The interpretation of the Genesis texts that has prevailed is therefore a male construct, acceptable to and indeed bound by the preconceptions of a patriarchal culture and specific to a time when male consciousness was taken as the human norm. The inherent contradictions in the story as well as the derogation of women presumed in its exegesis were handed on in ways that encouraged the perception of women and Nature as inferior, and at times, as in the persecution of witches, could be used to justify their terrorization. Had women had access to formal theological education and to spiritual authority, the bias and illogicality of canonized interpretations might have been exposed long before now, to the great benefit of women and men alike.

Therefore when today the issue of a different interpretation is raised, it comes at a time when, with the rise in women's consciousness and the beginnings of their acceptance as theologians, an unprecedented opportunity exists for a fresh and balanced view of these foundational texts, and consequently for their fruitful incorporation into a Christian ecological vision. By way of turning a metaphoric sword into a ploughshare, we would do well to rephrase the American Tract Society's ruling that "She who was first in the transgression must yet be the principal earthly instrument in the restoration," as "She who was first transgressed against may yet be the principal earthly instrument in the restoration of our relationship with the earth."

# 9

# Genesis from Outside the Box

How is this uncommon perception of Eve to come about? That is another way of asking what happens if we do not read the Genesis story of creation within the canonical constraints of the problematical doctrine of "original sin." What if we discard the box and look at its contents from an ecological perspective?

Some of the possibilities this offers have already been raised and were implicit in the close attention paid to what is actually contained in the text. This groundwork now enables me to propose some uncommon perceptions of the characters in the Genesis story and to ask what they contribute to an ecological Christian vision.

### Uncommon perceptions

First, the text offers us *an uncommon perception of man*. Instead of the hierarchical male of the standard interpretation, placed in power over his female dependents and over the earth, man shares with them the common clay and breath of all living beings. There is no reason to believe that his will, his intellect, or his body is by nature at the mercy of disordered sexual desire. He is not seduced by woman from a proper relationship with God. His sexuality is an intrinsic part of that relationship and of his interaction with other living beings. He is not set apart from them in his spirit or in his body. With them he shares a relationship with God, and along with them, shapes the world in which each is created mortal by nature. He gives names to all the other living beings, and woman he names as mother of all the living. He toils to produce food from the earth, and presumably obeys his

**109**

final and most solemn instruction from God — that he is to serve the earth, not the earth him. When he dies, he returns to that earth from which he came.

Second, it offers *an uncommon perception of woman*. Her behavior entails no suggestion of inferiority to the man. She opens the conversation with the serpent on behalf of both of them, judges for herself that the fruit is good to eat and will provide useful insight, and takes the initiative in eating it. Then she offers to share it with the man, and he accepts it from her, and both receive insight into the nature of good and evil. Are the consequences of this so terrible for them? God admits that once they have eaten the fruit, all that differentiates him from them is immortality. According to the first creation account, similarity to God was bestowed on male and female from the beginning, but in the garden story it is won from God: through the woman's action. The human race obtains self-awareness and the ability to exercise judgment and discretion. It has evolved into maturity and independence. Female fertility is celebrated by man as the source of all life in the world, and this life is sustained by eating the products of man's interaction with the earth's fertility.

Third, we gain *an uncommon perception of the serpent*. This representative of the animal world is a symbol of the wisdom offered to humankind in interaction with that world. This is the wisdom recorded and scrutinized in such Biblical books as Job, Qoheleth, Psalms, and Proverbs — texts that deal with the paradoxes of human existence and the harsh facts of life. (This will be considered in some detail in the final chapter.) The serpent exposes the complex problems involved in following fixed rules of conduct or imposed norms of behavior. At the interpersonal level, tension always marks the interface between individual self-realization and social norms. Any rules that promote helplessness should be resisted, for they operate by invoking penalties against self-reliance, competence and effectiveness. Even such supposedly divine prohibitions as those placed on knowledge or learning must be called into question.

The serpent also dramatizes the complexity of our relationships with the natural world. The woman personifies the potential consequences of those relationships. Do we utilize the insights offered by Nature as a pathway to a relationship with each other and with God? Where else do we expect to find these insights today?

Fourth, we are offered *an uncommon perception of God*. God appears as a generally benevolent though at times inflexibly severe male parent. He is kind enough to give his children life, a cozy existence, and suitable playmates, but in return he demands total obedience and exerts constant supervision. They are denied such basic human liberties as knowing right from wrong and freedom to choose between them. Since their obedience is secured by threats, like any normal child they respond by rebelling, even though this risks separation from the parent and with it the loss of physical and emotional comfort. This is the price of growing up. Liberation from coercion, especially religious coercion, is a central element of religious maturity.[1]

To those who object to bringing God down to the level of a parent, honesty compels a blunt response: a far greater objection is that he is portrayed here as a parent no human father or mother would adopt as a role model. He uses a classical "double-bind" method – a combination of favors and threats, carrots and sticks – in order to bend his offspring to his will.

At issue here is an extremely important insight into language about God. We may be tempted to reject anthropomorphic images of God out of hand without facing the fact that we cannot avoid using such images. The problem with this one is that it represents God as a *bad* human parent. Certainly God may be portrayed as a father, but not a *bad* father! Shaw's black girl is way ahead of the field here. God is a mother, certainly. But surely not a *bad* mother!

As we saw, one of the cornerstones of the "original sin" hypothesis was the desire to keep the goodness of God intact. To this end, any action less than perfect, or rather any so perceived, must be attributed to the serpent, the woman, or the man. Therefore it becomes axiomatic that whatever God does in the story is good; his actions are consistently read through rose-colored spectacles. By contrast, human and animal actions are read through sin-flecked lenses in an attempt to explain why it is that we suffer, inflict suffering, and die in pain. And because "sin" is projected on to all the characters in the drama except God, his actions are always assumed to be beyond reproach – even when patently they are not.

One might say that Christians who read the text in this way become like the inhabitants of James Hilton's lost valley of Shangri-La where everyone is blind. Those who enter must, if they wish to remain there, give up the gift of sight.

The alternative is to develop *an uncommon perception of sin*. We can take a first step by thinking about the Cain story, which presents good and evil as helping or harming one's fellow earth-creatures. The choice is made within one's own ecosystem and in interaction with those of others and their common relationship to God. It is no accident that the setting of Cain's sin involves the possession of certain products of the earth's fertility and their offering to God – an offering whose acceptance would ensure continued fertility.

It is therefore clear that I have not invented a new sin when with the theologians of the poor of this earth I talk about sinful structures or structural sin. Nor am I attributing a specific sin, the fault of Cain alone, to abstract, impersonal agricultural systems. The central problem today, as it was then, is the creation and maintenance of structures and centers of power, whether urban or rural, that effectively block all forms of loving our fellow earth-creatures whether in public, in our church practices, or in our homes. By and large, these structures prevent the recognition and growth of diversity, and foster an us-versus-them attitude that remains the very essence of sin. Just such an attitude made Cain, a herdsman, literally incapable of recognizing the gifts of the farmer. In the context of our worship of God, the same drive to exclusiveness has fostered hatred, division, and war. In the context of our relationship with the more-than-human world, it has led us to deny the intrinsic worth of the rest of creation.

A second step towards an uncommon perception of sin is to recognize that these structures have power on a global scale to enslave human beings, to make them their lives a misery, and to kill them. From this perspective, Abel was the first individual victim of an eco-war. Today, as we have seen, the tally reads in the millions, whether in Africa, Latin America, or the Ganges delta.

This step demands that we consider the mechanisms that turn us into participants in this sin. It is not just *outside* us, for unwillingly or unwittingly, we are involved in it as accomplices. This fact emerges time and time again from ecological studies of environmental problems with their quota of death, destruction, and suffering. One of the mechanisms is the relationship between us and hierarchical laws, including religious law. The inertia involved in living under the rule of law leads to sins of omission – tacitly accepting policies of exploitation against "them." Women understand this only too well. Hierarchical government operates by *power-over* at the cost of *power-from-within*. It sanctions sins against the Spirit; it devalues and destroys the diversity that creates ecological community and that fills the earth with glory.[2]

### Reperceiving God in Genesis

What God do we see now in the Genesis story? What happens if we do not take the goodness of God for granted, if we accept that in some mysterious way the oneness of the earth's systems and the oneness of God challenges us to think about God in the context of the human structural sin evident in those systems?

The first thing that happens is that we have to decide whether or not we really believe in the oneness of God. Judith Plaskow tackles this question in a discussion of Jewish monotheism. She tries to give voice to a new, inclusive monotheism that embraces and mirrors the diversity that we want to see honored in the world. The male monotheism that has shaped our common religious heritage is understood as the worship of God as Lord, as the king of all the earth. The imagery is exclusively masculine. Yet Plaskow does not want us to stop at the difficulties created at this level. If we were to call God "Queen of all the earth", it might perhaps soften and change the picture somewhat for those who have never heard of Boadicea or Maeve. But it does not alter the basic image of God as Dominating Other who drowns Egyptians in the sea and enforces obedience on children through a mixture of bribes and punishments. Feminists of either sex are not likely to want to worship such a deity any more than they do her male counterpart. From the issue of male terminology we must therefore move to that of the nature of this one God affirmed in monotheism.

Plaskow tackles this head on. She says that one of the things she has most valued about Judaism is its holistic understanding of God in relation to the problem of evil. (The book of Job, for example, wrestles with this problem.) A number of strands of Judaism have acknowledged that if God is the creator of the world, and the world contains pain, ambiguity, and evil, then these must have their origins in the same God who urges us to choose life and justice. Plaskow says, "I do not think that it is God's wrath alone that poses a special problem for feminists, but rather both mercy and wrath when these are meted out by an authoritarian parent trying to get human beings to do his will."[3]

Plaskow's honesty in wrestling with the monotheism of the biblical God of Judaism brings us back to the problems created by the Platonic notion of unity. Wiles puts the case succinctly. Although the Bible speaks in emphatic terms of God as one, he says, the concern of the biblical tradition is to repudiate all forms of polytheism and idol-worship, and thereby to underscore the teaching that there is only one God. It is with this teaching in all its complexity that Plaskow wrestles. What does it mean to say that this God knows good and evil? Does God know it in the same way as we do – as something inextricably bound up with the fact of being part of this world?

*I wonder too*

This leads us on to *an uncommon perception of Jesus and of incarnation*. Rather than attribute to him everything that is divine and transcendent, it forbids us to exclude from our understanding of Jesus any possibility of normal human weakness, limitation, or concession. What is required here is a deliberate step in the direction of recovering his total humanity, and with it the realization that he was, as much as we are, involved in sinful structures. He too was guilty of categorizing: the Jews are "us" and the pagans "them", as he told the Syro-Phoenician woman. He dealt with another "them", the Pharisees, in ways that provoked their enmity and sharpened conflicts with them. He derided them as hypocrites, who do exactly the opposite of the ideal he proclaimed with regard to dealing with one's enemies.

In his authentic historical context, because Jesus was polemical or ambiguous, he did not appear isolated from sin.[4] On the contrary, he was identified with it: "We *know* that this man is a sinner." (John 9:24) Therefore, as was said before, he did not die *for* sinners, but *with* sinners. To employ the terms of the Genesis story, his flesh suffered death not for everyone else's sins, nor even for his own, but because he was mortal.

Such a perception of Jesus has been operative throughout this book, for an ecological interpretation of his life does not isolate him from his environment or from the living earth systems that sustained him. It leaves open the paradox of incarnation, of the blending of humanity and divinity. One way Christian exegetes grappled with this paradox was, as we saw, to ignore it. By assuming that God is undifferentiated goodness (however you define that), all the problems with "badness" in the Genesis narrative were isolated from God and projected onto the other characters in the biblical story.

### An ecological reading of Genesis 1–3

But what if sin is not the proper interpretive category for this story? What if we assume instead that this story, like all the others in the Bible, arose in the context of a particular society in which the actions of certain individuals or groups in the story are consistent with the rules and values operative in that society? What if we place it in the context of a particular ecosystem, a set of interacting bodies, largely self-regulating but vulnerable and open to larger ones – both natural and human – all around? What if we read it not as a story of origins, but as a superlatively imaginative account of a particular group's faith in God?

In such an ecological reading, God is neither dictating the script nor directing the action to a foregone tragic conclusion. No one doubts whether or not he is onstage. He is certainly in the scene, a mysterious presence intimately related to the other three worlds in the story: animal, plant, and human. He is totally involved with the action, but since he cannot be pointed to and the other characters can, his involvement with them is measured in terms of how well they interact. His will is perceived as a proper order of relationships between them. So for a vegetarian society recounting the story the plants are his gift of food, remembered as such even when the script is written down in a later carnivorous society in which the animals may be eaten with his blessing.

In this society, men do the naming, the ordering, the plowing, the sowing, the weeding out of thorns and thistles, the sweaty labor of breaking new ground. Women are subject to their husbands, treated as Abraham's Sarah is treated, a body created to be his companion, to be blamed for his misfortunes, bartered for his survival or used to bear him a son. Such women fear barrenness; bear children in pain and anxiety; are anxious for their survival in the harsh conditions of an environment where plant, animal and child must vie with each other for water and sustenance.

When reread in the context of early Israelite society, the story becomes a revelation of human longing for integrity in its relationships with the world and with God. It also intimates how good life can be when those relationships are properly ordered. Above all, it is a story of what it means to be human, of what human nature is capable of, both positively and negatively.

It is also a story of how we wrestle with the mysterious notion of the oneness of God. How do we live with a God who creates a world of harmony and happiness but leaves within it the possibility of its destruction? How can we solve the puzzle of whether God's nature is good or bad – or both at once? Is God responsible for the suffering of those he creates or is he not? Does God give us the necessities for life at some times and withhold them at others, so that sometimes we are offered life and at other times death? Are life and death inextricably bound together, different sides of the same coin? Is God someone who forces obedience on us through a mixture of bribes and punishments? If God is the creator of the world, and the world contains pain, ambiguity and evil, then these must have their origins in God at the same time that God urges us to choose life and justice.

Read this way, the story gives expression to an inclusive monotheism that embraces and mirrors the diversity of experience of God in a particular time and place. It presupposes God's responsibility for the whole of creation and therefore God's relationship with each and every part of it. It leaves us with the picture of ourselves embedded in all the other systems that make up the organic whole we call earth.

Once we surmount the barrier of later derogatory perceptions of Eve, the way is open to seeing the narrative as it existed in Israel before the emergence of the influential expositions of Jewish and Christian antiquity. Recognizing that the ancient biblical texts reflect the world of the late second or early first millennium BCE, and that conditions in that world were different from those in later times, we can discover the Eve that existed before her prototypical linkage with sin and suffering.

This Eve existed in a Palestinian setting where "Eden" was a longed-for place of continuously flowing waters, where the constant fear of drought would be lifted from the anxious shoulders of Israelite farmers. According to Genesis 2:5, life was not possible without the two critical elements of rainfall and human labor. Until Yahweh caused a stream to water the land, and until he formed an earthling to work the earth, there could be neither bush nor sprouting grain. Just before humanity is created (Gen 2:7), the lack of water and workers means there is no food, and just afterwards (Gen 2:9), God has made the conditions for food available. The creation of humanity is the middle step in this process, and the whole passage is telling us that human existence is inextricably caught up with concern for sustenance. The Israelite highlanders, confronted with the daily reality of intensive labor, were naturally drawn to the idea that life might be otherwise. Hence the narrative allows a brief glimpse of the ephemeral state of Eden, and then brings humans into the real world.

While sustenance alone would be sufficient for animals, recognition of an intrinsic human need for more than mere survival is present in the phrase which tells us that the trees are "pleasing to the eye." The creative sequence has neared completion when we are told that the earthling finds no helper. In Hebrew this word can refer to a superior as well as an inferior – in Psalm 121:1–2 it characterizes God, to whom one turns in distress. The prepositional phrase "as his partner" that appears in Genesis 2:18 and 20 tells us what kind of helper is meant here. It establishes a non-hierarchical relationship between the two. It means "opposite," "corresponding to," "parallel with," "on a par with."[5] Yahweh casts the earthling into a comatose state, far closer to original non-existence than ordinary sleep, and the creative sequence is completed with the differentiation of human life when woman, the helping partner, is formed.

In this context, what can be the basic thematic element of the Eden story if it is not sin? The answer is to be found in the vocabulary and word usage. The language that dominates the narrative must be taken as significant and intentional. Especially in the case of biblical narratives that would have been recited to attentive audiences, the repetition of key words and phrases is a characteristic means by which Hebrew literature emphasizes important objects and ideas. In non-literate cultures, verbatim repetition, in particular the reiteration of individual words, is a common device for stressing motifs. This device usually disappears in translations into modern languages where style and idiom are impatient of such repetition.

One such "theme word" in the Genesis narrative is the common root from which the verb "eat" and the noun "food" developed. (Earlier we noted a similar situation in the translation of 'adam.) Such repetition is lost when languages – like English in this case – do not have a cognate noun and verb. The Hebrew root word in question here is 'kl, "to eat." In these two chapters it recurs in one form or another more frequently than any other word except *'adam.* Its appearance at key places in the narrative draws attention to pivotal features of the action. According to Genesis 2:16, the very first words that a living human being hears – those of the Lord God saying, "You may eat freely of every tree of the garden" – concern the existence of a food supply. The striking repetition and placement carry their own message: the beginning of human existence coincides with a search for sustenance. Original human consciousness, as defined in this story, consists of two vital aspects: the ability to relate to God so as to understand God's instructions about our relationship with the earth, and the human need to know about the sources of food.[6]

This very simple fact has been forgotten or is overlooked in cultures where the means of sustenance are abundant. In our industrialized consumer society, the consumption of food is largely taken for granted. We scarcely notice shelves filled with delicacies and yearn rather for money, power, or sexual gratification. Small wonder that we read the references to sustenance in this narrative on a full stomach and so miss their significance. For this is a very different experience from hearing it or reading it on an empty one, a condition that was probably quite usual for those who first gave voice to its drama and those who listened to them. For them, food was not a literary device for introducing the concept of disobedience, even if we mistakenly so understand it. Eating was a central issue in itself, a literally gnawing concern about the availability of sustenance. The story attests to the integral relationship between this sustenance and the difficulties of securing it.

These difficulties are recognized in the speeches to the woman and man in Genesis 3:16–19, where the inevitable cycle of birth, toil, and death is given the sanction of divine will. They recognize the difficult nature of humanity's intrinsic connection to the ground, for in order to store winter rain and summer dew, the early inhabitants of the Palestinian highlands had to carve cisterns out of the bedrock that lay close to the surface of the hilltops on which most of the early villages were located. Whether done with bronze or iron tools, this required monumental expenditures of labor.

Besides the fluctuating pattern of annual rainfall, the Israelites also faced the constraints imposed on agriculture by the mountainous terrain, hardly the easiest place to plant and grow barley. The scarcity of level ground led to the construction of terraces, a number of which archaeologists have dated to the period of earliest Israelite settlement. This deceptively simple technological device made all the difference. It allowed the creation of fields, gardens and vineyards on slopes otherwise too rocky or

steep for anything but thorns and scrub oak to grow. But extensive terracing
required a huge expenditure of human energy, a staggering investment of
time and labor And terraces needed to be maintained against flooding and
erosion. A suprafamily collective labor system would have been necessary.

For women, the increased labor demand posed a double burden. More
work meant more women employed in the back-breaking labor of building
and repairing walls and other defenses against erosion. But increased labor
also called for a larger work force, which in turn called for larger families.
Thus the endless burdens of highland dry farming rested on the shoulders
of both women and men and on the reproductive capacity of women.[7]
Small wonder then that the river valley environments and the flat stretches
of arable land to the East in Mesopotamia provided a picture of Eden!

While I was enjoying Carol Meyers' absorbing account of archaeologi-
cal digs and analyses of Israelite life at the beginning of the Iron Age (the
time setting she thinks most likely for the Genesis narrative), I happened to
see a program on agriculture in China that showed canals, terracing, and the
intensive manual labor of men and women alike. Reporters gave statistics
and other information about deaths from famine following on crop failure
or flooding. It brought home to me the basic problem we in the developed
world have with the Genesis text. We no longer work in order to eat in order
to live. Food is only an item in the family budget, often a relatively small
one.

Yet the integral relationship between sustenance, the difficulties of
securing it, and forging human relationships with the more-than-human
world around us are the interpretive grid through which, as ecology reminds
us, this narrative has once again become relevant today. The ecological slogan, "There is no such thing as a free lunch" is just another way of reading
the judgments of God in Genesis 3:16f. Sadly, the way we live keeps us deaf
to this message, whether we encounter it in the Bible or in ecological slo-
gans.

---

*Handwritten marginalia (top):* The problem with good & evil is that they are both static, whereas we live in a world that is constantly changing. Moreover, time and space fracture good, so there is no possibility of choosing only "good". It will always be qualified by time and space.

*Handwritten marginalia (left):* where and when set the limits of one's choice for "good". Goodness can take place only at the intersection of time and space. Good + evil are terms that can be most aptly applied to emerging consciousness—the greater one's consciousness the less applicable the terms are—if preserving my impulse here is it's good? or the other is "bad"?

*Handwritten marginalia (bottom):* there is no such thing as good and evil within nature—only within creation that "good" and evil appear—of necessity—because us to make choices—time and space applies only in the human realm.

# 10

# Ecological Humility

In the opening chapter I drew attention to the role and importance of modesty in making any claim to know what God knows, or indeed in any claim to know God. By their very nature, immodest claims ignore the essential difference between divine and human knowledge. The difference lies between what we claim to know about God or what God knows, and what God actually knows. Only God knows that.

### From theological modesty

In the Genesis narrative, the serpent characterizes God as one who knows good and evil. The serpent, it appears, knows more about God than Eve does. Instead of resenting this implied deficiency in her knowledge, she learns from the serpent. This ability to learn about God from the more-than-human world depends on respect for those who belong to it and for what they know. With that respect, we too may learn from them. But whatever we may learn, our knowledge remains within human limits.

Such readiness to learn lies at the heart of what is now generally understood as scientific progress. God's call for Job to recognize his ignorance, when responded to in the spirit of scientific inquiry, has certainly increased our knowledge of "the foundation of the earth. . . of its measurement. . . of the storehouses of snow. . . of when the mountain goats bring forth." (Job 38–39) But such knowledge has also taken us, time and again, to the boundaries of human understanding.

We may react to this limitation with modesty in the face of our ignorance, or with arrogance that ignores it. Ideally, we recognize our ignorance, and any modest claim to knowledge on our part remains just that. Arne Naess' response to the greatness of the mountain, recognizing his comparative small-ness and so coming nearer to participating in that greatness, is exemplary here. Coming nearer to its greatness without appropriating that to ourselves main-tains the boundaries between us and the mountain, and between what we know of the mountain and what the mountain "knows" – of itself or of us.

Those of us, however, with access neither to mountains nor serpents, nor with any declared scientific intent, still need to be critically aware of what we learn from the more-than-human world. Speaking to a horticultural meeting in Minnesota in 1947 on the philosophy of gardening, artist Clare Leighton declared herself "an amateur before an expert audience." The horticulturists, she said, knew the different families of flowers and all about them whereas she was simply "a lover of working in the earth." As such, she focused on our attitude toward the earth and toward our gardens. What matters is not what we do to our gardens, but what our gardens do to us, she said, for no one who has confronted a garden can help recognizing that we are its servants and not its masters. And that is "an extremely good feeling. It is an especially good feeling today when man is inclined, in this scientific age, to be rather too arro-gant."[1]

Here we note a compelling echo of God's final command to Adam and Eve in the Genesis narrative: "Serve the earth from which you were taken." Do we, like Clare Leighton, see ourselves as its servants? Can we be content to learn something about ourselves from it rather than assume we are its mis-tresses? Above all, are we humble enough to accept that as earthlings we are indeed "taken from it?" To recognize this is to move from theological mod-esty to ecological humility, from being modest in our claims about what we know to being humble in our claims about what we are.

### To ecological humility

These two aspects of our response to earth and its more-than-human inhabitants are, of course, linked. But I want to concentrate first on what we think we are compared to earth's other inhabitants. Some years ago I was asked to give a public lecture in a series entitled, "Let Me Enjoy the Earth!" My first reaction to the title was one of disbelief, for it sounded to me like the cry of a spoiled child: "Let me *enjoy* myself!" But upon checking on the source of the title, I learned that it came from the opening verse of one of Thomas Hardy's "Country Songs":

Let me enjoy the earth no less
Because the all-enacting Might

That fashionèd forth its loveliness
Had other aims than my delight.[2]

*[handwritten marginal note: Don't be a spoiled child – ecological humility]*

Reading the whole poem, I no longer heard the voice of a spoiled child. I heard instead one that we badly need to listen to today. Hardy is saying, in no uncertain terms, that *our* enjoyment of the earth is not the primary aim of its creation, because what he calls "the all-enacting Might that fashioned forth its loveliness" had, and presumably still has, other aims than *human* delight. For me this expresses perfectly the concept of ecological humility: accepting our place *within* the whole earth household rather than acting as if God had conferred "most favored species" status on us. That attitude in fact colors most of our behavior most of the time. We think and act as if all the other members of that household have no other aim than to serve our aims – as if, in Leighton's phrase, we are its masters and its very existence is ordained by God to serve our pleasure.

I don't know how Hardy's poem was received in his lifetime. I do know how its sentiments would be received today. For instance, when the latest statistics on human world population and their dire effects on global ecosystems and biodiversity are published, the *New York Times*, *Daily Telegraph*, *USA Today*, *The Guardian* or the *Washington Post* would not be likely to print Hardy's poem as a politically or theologically correct response. I don't know if Hardy himself was aware of it, but in 1801 Britain had fewer than 11 million people; yet by 1891, when he was in his forties, the population was 33 million. Today we know that the British number over 58 million, and that Britain is one of the few European countries expecting a population increase – to about 61.5 million in 2023.

Few people seem concerned that in forty years the world's human population has more than doubled – from 3 billion in 1960 to over 6 billion in 2004 – and that this is connected to the extinction of other species. This is generally ignored except by a relatively small group of people, many of them specialists in various scientific fields. The enormity of scale is itself a barrier to understanding what it means. Who can visualize three billion people, never mind double that number? And whatever glimpse we might have of the consequences of this massive increase, in particular of the human and non-human suffering attached to them, could itself deter us from seeking to know more about such grim outcomes.

My immediate concern is the way in which theologies of creation, and especially of revelation, have contributed to a lack of concern about the size of the human population and its effects on the "flesh" of earthly life within which we are embedded. In large part they have done so by fostering the attitude that we have a God-given right to enjoy the earth and its resources, and hang the consequences – even for ourselves. This means that we cannot accept the reality expressed in Hardy's poem. We cannot bear the thought that the divine aims in creation may not be the same as ours. Above all, we cannot bear the thought that God's purposes may run directly contrary to ours.

Others, however, have faced this unpalatable truth. The Babylonian Talmud contains a pertinent comment on the triumph song memorializing the Israelites' safe passage across the Red Sea: "I will sing to the Lord! Glorious his triumph! Horse and rider he has cast into the sea!" (Exod 15:1) Then, says the Talmud, a voice comes from heaven: "How can I rejoice when my creatures are perishing?" The biblical writers assume that God's concern does not extend to the Egyptians, but the Talmudic challenge to that assumption comes from within Judaism itself. However shocking that was and still is, how much more shocking would it be to extend God's concern from the Egyptian riders to the horses? Yet the Talmudic text does allow the possible reading, "How can I enjoy myself when *any* of my creatures are perishing?"

This resonates with a nuance in Hardy's implied question: "Is *my* enjoyment of the earth lessened because God intends others too to enjoy it?" Both questions force us to face the self-centeredness of our assumptions about who and what matters to God. Above all, it forces us to look at how traditional theologies of salvation presume and at the same time reinforce the presumption that ultimately we alone matter to God.

### What ecological humility requires

I want to challenge that assumption by describing in some detail what ecological humility (inextricably linked to theological modesty) requires of us. Ecology, as I said in chapter five, is a scientific discipline that investigates the intimate and essential relationships between all members of the earth household according to specific interconnections proper to their home ecosystem. Thus, for instance, the interconnections between entities within a marine ecosystem will differ in some important respects from those within a mountain environment. But it also recognizes the ultimate interdependence – though on different timescales and according to differing criteria – of each ecosystem with all others and ultimately with the whole earth system. These relationships are characterized by interaction and interdependence at a variety of levels.

Ecology therefore employs a systems approach in its analysis of the character and function of relationships within different types of ecosystem; but it does so while emphasizing the whole system over its parts, and the processes over its structure. (Such processes as negative and positive feedback loops, for example, posit a circular arrangement of causally connected elements, in which each has an effect on the next, until the last "feeds back" the effect into the first element of the cycle.) And not only do timescales vary, but such important global systems as those involved in climate change operate on a timescale that far exceeds the past two thousand years of human history.[3]

Briefly then, human ability to exist and to act in freedom depends on the longevity, endurance, mutability, and stability of the natural ecosystems in which our human communities are embedded. This modifies the concept of human freedom to one of freedom exercised in awareness of interdependence, for the effects on the wider earth community of exercising that freedom must be taken into account. Our interdependence becomes a vital factor in human decision-making as we begin to recognize the concrete ecological exigencies of human life as vital elements of an internally connected moral order that embraces the whole earth household .[4]

Ecologically as well as theologically, then, all our interrelationships and those with whom we share them count as part of an interconnected physical and spiritual order. Theologically as well as ecologically, therefore, we can no longer see our salvation – defined in terms of our capacity for dignity, well-being, and happiness – as in any real sense separate from that of the whole Earth household. How we live affects all its members, and even when measured along different timescales, their lives affect ours. Most humbling must be the realization that while they got along perfectly well without us for some billions of years, and could do so again, we could not survive without them. Human independence is a political, not a biological concept.

### Theology, ecology and humility

Still, this growth in ecological consciousness among the members of the scientific community finds little resonance in traditional theology, because such awareness requires a revolutionary change in theological self-perception. We are asked to turn from self-centered relationships with both the earth and God to one based on our membership and participation in the earth household. The theological demands this alteration entails are vividly expressed by Brecht in his play *Galileo.* Faced with the implications of the Copernican revolution that demands a radical change in our perception of the relationship between earth and sun, an old cardinal cries out, "I won't have it! I won't have it! I won't be a nobody on an inconsequential star briefly twirling hither and thither." Not only is the earth the center of all things for him, but, he asserts, "I am the center of the earth, and the eye of the Creator falls on me, and me alone." The lesser lights of the stars and the great light of the sun were created, he cries, "to give light upon me that God might see me – humankind, God's greatest effort, the center of creation."[5]

But Hardy's poem, which constitutes a positive response to the

Copernican revolution, inspires in some a similar dread – the dizzying fear that if we lose the sense of personal significance that arises from being placed by God at the centre of creation, then we shall indeed no longer matter to God or to each other: we shall become "inconsequential nobodies."

This fear lies behind all-too-predictable responses to any suggestion that we need to change our perception of our being the most significant species on earth. Such a proposal is typically met with, "Oh, you don't care about human beings! You care more about lapwings (or hopping mice, whales, toads, rainforests, gorillas)!" But ecology teaches us that it is not a question of caring more, but of caring differently. It means seeing ourselves not as isolated at the center of creation and somehow insulated from what happens to the rest of it, but of enlarging our area of concern to the earth household that encompasses our lives. Ultimately, of course, its well-being is very much our concern.

This rather utilitarian approach prompts and supports an ecologically humble lifestyle. It becomes explicitly theological when it helps us to take seriously the insight that God is similarly concerned with the whole of creation, with the Egyptian as well as the Israelite, the horse as well as the rider. The cardinal speaks for traditional theologies that presuppose that God's gaze is focused on us, and that the rest of creation is therefore peripheral to God's solicitude. We alone, he presumes, are actively involved in that relationship; we alone are able to express and develop it. In short, we communicate with God on behalf of the world. Everything, as the cardinal says, depends on us and our responses. Surely God must have been gratified when on the eve of the millennium we floodlit churches and cathedrals – even though the spike in energy consumption elevated carbon emissions, global warming rose another notch and penguin and polar bear habitats crumbled into the rising sea.

This ecclesiastical millennium celebration shows that the cardinal's theology is alive and well today. Its healthy state relies in no small part on a doctrine of revelation that excludes all other life forms from the possibility of God being revealed to them and of their responding to that revelation. But what does this imply about God? The mantra of this theology runs as follows: "God has revealed to us alone on earth that God is revealed to us alone." This circular proposition in regard to revelation keeps us firmly inside the canonical box – and the lid tightly closed. Thinking ourselves to be the only ones inside may do much to bolster our self-importance, but it does nothing to safeguard the majesty and glory of a God who laid the very foundations of the earth.

An increasing number of written and visual descriptions of Earth's evolution are giving us a riveting account of the physical, chemical, and geological processes that formed the planet over vast timescales before our species emerged.[6] They raise important theological questions: How can we imagine that God's relationship with the earth household began only with our emergence? Who are *we* to confine God's involvement to such a minuscule span in earth's history? On what grounds may we confidently assert (not in all humility, but rather with none at all) that God did not communicate with any creature until one with a human voice could respond? Did we not rather emerge out of an existing relationship between God and our planet that characterizes the long, variegated history of the whole earth household?

The Epistle to the Hebrews begins by affirming that while long ago, God spoke to people through the prophets, "in these last days God has spoken to *us* in Jesus Christ." (Heb 1:1, my italics) Does this allow for a different kind of communication with all the species who preceded us? Or do we suppose that God had to hang around waiting for some kind of dialogue with creation until we showed up? Would not the God of Job laugh this to scorn?

### God's revelation

The Jewish scholar and mystic Franz Rozenzweig shows proper reverence for God and for the divine capacity for revelation by stressing its sequence. He says:

> God spoke. That came third.
> It was not the first thing.
> The first thing was: God created.
> God created the earth and the skies.
> That was the first thing.
>
> The breath of God moved over the face of the waters:
> over the darkness covering the face of the deep.
> That was the second thing.
>
> Then came the third thing.
> God spoke.[7]

This sequence, common to biblical and scientific accounts, shows that God was not first revealed through speech. From "the beginning" God was and is revealed through the processes of creating through the evolution of the planet: its atmosphere, its life, its species. Here, in Rozenzweig's phrase, "the shell of the mystery breaks." And as it breaks, God's self is expressed, revealed through the processes we call evolution.

To whom, or to what is God's self revealed? To every living creature that emerges through coevolutionary processes and responds to God "according to its kind." But not with words. The morning stars sang together, the heavens recited the glory of God, but *no speech, no words, no voice was heard* (Ps 19:3, my italics).

This recognition of the continuous nature of revelation and of every living being's response to it requires both ecological humility and theological modesty. It proposes that God's self is revealed through more than human words, and that that revelation did not have to wait until there was a human voice to utter and a human ear to hear; until a human intelligence could interpret and a human hand record; until a human response acknowledged the mystery of God's self-expression.

Traditional theologies and doctrines of salvation suppose precisely the opposite; this opposite is encapsulated in the creedal statement, "For us men and for our salvation he [Jesus] came down from heaven." The insistent theological formula *"for us"* has legitimated the traditional assumption that all other species are excluded from salvation, from divine revelation, from Paradise. The liturgical repetition as well as the theological presupposition of that formula has canonized the Christian exclusionary principle by which all other species are deemed without value except in their usefulness and service to us. In this way, traditional Christian theologies of revelation and salvation have nurtured and reinforced the formula's latent arrogance about our role and place within the earth community.

They have also done so by reinforcing a hierarchically vertical view of ourselves and of earth: one in which God reigns above angels, men and women in descending order of importance and value, with earth and its creatures permanently below or beneath them. The metaphoric power of the language of dominance based on this valuation system legitimates human dominance over all that lies "beneath" us – particularly the "ground" that supports the material household of life. So like the cardinal, we react with discomfort to language that demotes us from our exalted position by describing us as the servants of earth rather than its mistresses.

In that hierarchical evaluation, Earth is merely a place where we, and we alone, may (temporally) know, love, and serve God; and if saved, earn an eternal reward in heaven by doing so. Earth's intrinsic value in the sight of God is implicitly negated or at best, greatly diminished. And so is our flesh, the material substance of which we are made; for, it is supposed, we "know" God only through the immaterial, spiritual part of our nature. And as we alone are presumed to possess this, then we alone are presumed capable of knowing God. Revelation happens, as it were, only in and on our terms.

In such ways, the traditional theology of salvation keeps us "boxed" within these presuppositions about ourselves, unable to go outside it to where a different vision of God, ourselves, and earth awaits. But we need more than

knowledge to take that step outside. We need to learn and to practice the ecological humility that readily acknowledges our oneness with, rather than our
separation from, all members of the earth household – and enables us to see
them as having an earlier claim to knowledge of God.

In the Gospel of Thomas, Jesus is credited with teaching us this lesson:

> If your leaders tell you,
> Look! This presence is in the skies!
> Remember,
> the birds who fly the skies have known this all along.
> If they say,
> It is in the seas!
> remember,
> the dolphins and fish have always known it (Thom 3).

Such humble awareness of God's continuous revelation to the whole
Earth household accepts and welcomes whatever response each creature
makes to it according to its kind. This does not, obviously, exclude revelation
of God's mysterious presence through Jesus, nor make it less important to
those to whom it is offered. But it does put us in our proper place within the
household of life. At the same time it gives God God's proper place: it gives
God room to be God of the whole universe and of the community of life on
earth. "Where is all, there all should be."

The human arrogance evident in traditional views of revelation consists
in the fact that by claiming for ourselves the sole capacity on earth to receive
the full revelation of God, we deny that capacity in others. The ultimate theological arrogance is that we also deny or at best ignore God's capacity to
reveal the mystery of God's self to the whole earth, to all its inhabitants and
ultimately, to the universe. If human constraints and exclusion clauses set
bounds to how, when, and to whom God's will can be revealed, it is no longer
God's revelation. As Hardy discerned, in intent if not in effect we claim that
God's aims correspond to our own. We forget that God's thoughts are not
our thoughts, nor God's ways our ways, nor our speech the sole measure or
medium of God's voice. As if, indeed, it could be!

Job's instructions to Zophar put us firmly back in our place among those
who learn about God from the more-than-human members within the earth
household:

> But ask the beasts, and they will teach you;
> the birds of the air, and they will tell you;
> or the plants of the earth, and they will teach you;
> and the fish of the sea will declare to you.

> Who among all these does not know that the hand of the Lord
>     has done this?
> In God's hand is the life of every living thing
>     and the breath of all humankind (Job 12:7).

Eve, after all, was taught about God by the serpent. I am not saying that the mystery we call God has not been revealed to us through human language, nor that what has been revealed about God in and by the life of Jesus is not central for Christians. I am saying that we cannot reduce the whole of that revelation, in which the shell of God's mystery breaks, to what has been expressed to us, or by us; nor indeed can we reduce that expression to what has been said by or to a particular group of human beings at any particular time or place. I am saying that all life forms that emerged, flourished, and died in the eons before and since our emergence were and are created capable of knowing God according to their kind. And they are fully entitled to enjoy the earth, their home, according to their kind.

This being so, we have to think seriously about what our overwhelming presence today means for them, and what their ever-increasing loss means for God, as well as for ourselves. We have to pray and work for and, hopefully, find the humility and courage expressed in Hardy's final verse:

> And some day hence, toward Paradise
> And all its blest — if such should be —
> I will lift glad, afar-off eyes,
> Though it contain no place for me.[8]

What greater contrast than this could we find to the image of human salvation associated with the God enthroned above the great pillars of the "fall and redemption" doctrine? And how do we change our thinking about ourselves sufficiently to move outside the pale of their false security? The following chapter looks at some of the difficulties involved in that move, and also at the reassuring fact that by our very nature we are not only capable of change, but necessarily geared towards it.

# 11

# The Christian Gene

At the conclusion of the previous chapter we were confronted by the contrast between the security offered by the pillars of a "fall and redemption" theology and the uncertainty involved in moving away from them to an ecologically humble and theologically modest one. Seen in that way, the problem appears to be one of losing the stability and support those "pillars" have offered us and that we have invested in them over the centuries. Put simply, Christians have long been assured that the structure built around them offers a guarantee of salvation from sin, a warrant that is now, and ever shall be, impregnable to change or notable variation. The emphasis on its unchanging nature harks back to the canonical, self-reinforcing claim we examined in chapter six – namely, that all Christians have believed this, at all times and everywhere.

But Evelyn Fox-Keller's book, *The Century of the Gene*, puts that view of salvation and that claim in rather a different light. It does so by looking at a comparable phenomenon within science: the search for the gene as a unit of stability within species. The analogy with the perceived function of the Christian canonical "gene" became clear as I read her account of the relationship over the past century between the study of Darwinian evolution and the study of genetics. There appeared to be intriguing resemblances between the driving force behind their historic relationship and that which has driven traditional Christian theologies of salvation. Her opening chapter, for example, describes the search for the gene as the "regulator" of genetic stability. Also of interest is her subsequent point that today, when the word "gene" is common linguistic currency throughout western culture, there is little scientific consensus about what the entity so labeled actually is or does. In fact, she says, it may be "a concept past its time."

What particularly interests me, however, is Fox-Keller's disclosure of the presuppositions behind the search for the gene. The different chronological frameworks employed by evolution and genetics play important roles in their assumptions and conclusions. In popular as well as scientific culture, Darwin's theory of evolution through natural selection is associated with changes in biological form and function occurring over eons of geological time. Genetics, on the other hand, is concerned with the unmistakable stability and reproducibility of type within the evolution of species over relatively short spans of genealogical time. Geological time refers to the evolution of the earth's crust over 4.6 billion years; human genealogies, as generally understood, are reckoned over no more than some few hundred thousand years.

This contrast in time span is important, and I shall return to it. Here I want to focus, as Fox-Keller does, on the genealogy of the two sciences themselves. Genetics emerged after, indeed out of Darwin's work. It did so in large part because Darwin's theory of evolution through natural selection acting upon individual variation effectively did away with the fixity of species. After that, as she points out, it was no longer possible for the scientifically literate to believe in this fixity. Yet Darwin left them (and us) with the fact that we also see remarkable stability of type within species and persistence of particular individual features from generation to generation.

Viewed from the perspective of geological time, species transform and evolve. Yet viewed from the perspective of historical time, they display an unmistakable stability in form and function.[1]

Darwin was not unaware of this stability. But as is the case with research, he had to focus his energies. His primary project was to study the mechanisms of transformation within species over the vast and then practically incalculable span of geological time. His aim was to remedy our profound ignorance of "the laws of variation"; he left it to his heirs to discover the "laws of constancy." And as they applied themselves to this task they created the science now known as genetics. Both laws, however, influence the evolution of living beings.

### The search for the gene: the search for stability

To a large extent, Fox-Keller says, the search for the "laws of constancy" became a search for a hereditary unit so stable that its stability can account for the reliability with which traits are transmitted through generations. In other words, the problem of trait stability was answered by assuming the existence of an inherently stable, potentially immortal, unit that could be transferred intact through the generations.[2]

The search ended, or so it seemed, when the hereditary unit in question (now universally known as the gene) or, more precisely, its (DNA) was triumphantly displayed to the world by Watson and Crick in 1953. The term itself had been coined in 1909 – subsequent to the rediscovery in 1900 of Mendel's rules of inheritance – to refer to a hypothetical entity essential in the study of heredity. It was, for many scientists, analogous to the fundamental units of physics and chemistry, though no serious student thought of it as literally an atom. But however genes were understood, they were notional entities with an inherent capacity for faithful transmission from generation to generation. Then as now, "gene" and "generation" could hardly be more closely linked, either linguistically or imaginatively.

Fox-Keller makes an all-important point about the search for the gene as a mechanism of stability. From the time the gene was first hypothesized until its discovery as a physical entity, she says, the search was driven by the fact that scientists generally accepted Darwin's mechanisms of transformation. The evidence for their existence was sufficient to make the search for a mechanism of preservation a matter of urgency. The concept of the gene originated, as it were, as a reaction to Darwin's discovery that we, too, are subject to the laws of variation. It became imperative to demonstrate, indeed to reassure ourselves, that specific mechanisms ensure that we and our descendants remain recognizably the same over time. The Christian analogue, of course, is the proclaimed stability of the canonized account of human salvation transmitted through apostolic succession, apparently without change or variation.

Yet today, according to biologist Lynn Margulis, the received wisdom about the relationship between mechanisms of transformation and preservation within living beings is that we change in order to stay the same. Constant interaction between mechanisms of stability and mechanisms of change is essential for life – which might therefore be defined as a state of dynamic equilibrium between stability and change. It is not accidental that this understanding of their relationship is expressed paradoxically, for to say we change in order to stay the same subverts the usual understanding of both sameness and change. But the necessary interaction between the two opposing mechanisms means that this is just one of the paradoxes yielded by the study of heredity.

Yet all of us, scientist and non-scientist alike, resist not only the notion but also the experience of continual change. We look for constancy and stability in relationships; we rely substantially on it in our daily lives, and routinely commit ourselves to achieving some measure of it in our work. Fickleness, inconsistency and unreliability are all negative terms. Christians pray for eternal rest as a desired state for their loved ones after death. Nonetheless, the laws of variability and reactions to them manifest themselves to us and in us as biological phenomena that affect the lives of individuals and groups in a variety of ways. And generally speaking, whether as individuals or as groups, we react to them by reinforcing those elements that produce stability and constancy.

This explains to some degree the scale of shock and disquiet generated by Darwin's claim that like all other species, ours is subject to the laws of variation. It meant that we cannot, any more than other species, claim fixity of form for ourselves. For to do so would imply not only that we were entirely outside the evolutionary process common to all other life forms, but also that there was a "fixed" moment in time when we emerged as a species on earth. The fact that some of us were and still are ready to make both these immodest claims, and why this happens, is what this book is all about.

But to return to the immediate reactions to Darwin's theory: I am not saying that its implications were immediately obvious to the general public or that they were voiced in words as plain as mine. Still, they played a part, however inchoate, in the reaction to his findings. It is small wonder that in the western world, at least, the discovery that genes can function as agents of stability from generation to generation was a profoundly powerful one. Its power proceeded in no small measure from its being perceived as a guarantor of stable bloodlines, life forms, and character traits. In performing the work of both replication and conservation, it appeared to offer a guaranteed fidelity of self-replication over many generations.

### Does DNA provide species fixity?

"Or so it seemed," adds Fox-Keller. For the primary operative assumption was that DNA is an intrinsically stable molecule. That, in large measure, is why its discovery was accompanied by an extraordinary sense of satisfaction. Since the beginning of the twentieth century, she says, the notion of the gene as a self-replicating entity that carried the secret of its immortality in its very structure had been a staple of genetics. An actual chemical substance, already known to be a basic constituent of chromosomes, appeared to have the necessary defining properties.[3]

However, as she goes on to show, the confidence of scientists who declared that it remained only "to iron out the details" proved premature, if not unfounded. One surprise awaiting them bears directly on the gene as a source of stability through self-replication. Contrary to expectations, it has become clear that the structure of DNA provides only the beginnings of an explanation for this high fidelity. In fact, left to its own devices, DNA cannot even copy itself. Replication simply will not proceed in the absence of the enzymes required to carry out the process. Moreover, DNA is not intrinsically stable: its integrity is maintained by a panoply of proteins involved in forestalling or repairing copying mistakes, spontaneous breakage and other kinds of damage incurred in the process of replication.

In fact, then, DNA is not an aloof, metabolically inert material, but one maintained and exquisitely balanced in an actively supported environment. The stability of genes is now seen to be not so much a matter of molecular "statics" as one of biochemical dynamics dependent on vulnerable and unreliable parts. Genetic stability within living organisms is part of and cannot be isolated from mutability. Stability *and* mutability create and participate in the dynamic equilibrium characteristic of living organisms. Under cellular regulation their delicate balance shifts in response to the particular environment in which the cell finds itself. Life requires not just a rapidly changing set of self-replicating albeit error-prone nucleic acid molecules, but also their interaction with a metabolic, autocatalytic system specializing in self-maintenance.[4]

### The search for fixity in Christian theology

What has any of this to do with Christian theology? Or to put the question another way, why did the most immediate and vociferous rejection of Darwin's theories come from within Christianity? And why do some Christians still reject them outright today? Now that the mutable aspects of the gene are taken for granted, why do Christians in particular react so strongly to the notion of change in our genome? For indeed within western culture the scientific resistance to the notion of inter-generational mutability of species cannot compare with the resistance mounted by Christians. What do they in particular find threatening about the loss of fixity of species?

This is where I found Fox-Keller's analysis so enlightening. She is clear that what was intuitively sought for in the gene was a fundamental unit of stability transmitted from generation to generation, a unit that is potentially immortal. The analogy with Christianity is not in the search itself, but in the hypothesis behind it. For Christians have long believed, and many still do, that they have already found or been given that fundamental unit of stability, and that it has been given them by God. This belief is built on the assumption that as a group (not as a species) Christians have been given an analogous "hereditary" unit whose divinely ordained function is to make them potentially immortal. For just as the ultimate goal of human manipulation of the genetic code is often presented as saving us from "premature" death caused by disease, so too is the Christian "salvation gene" presented as saving us from death caused by sin or spiritual disease. "Salvation" is derived from the Latin *salus (health)*, which signifies not only "wellness," but also "security" and "safety."

### Salvation, Augustine's Christian gene

The safety in question is absolute: safety from death in both its physical and spiritual form. For those who claim possession of a particular form of this gene, physical death is not, as we have seen, part of a natural process, but something imposed on us by God as punishment for sin. On this Augustinian hypothetical base, the notional Christian gene is built up out of interlocking elements or complementary concepts. They follow the rules of base-pairings by which bi-polar units are constructed: in this instance, salvation and sin; Christ and Adam; life and death. Salvation, Christ, and life are seen as belonging together and are often used interchangeably, as are their polar opposites sin, Adam, and death. For in Christianity the term "salvation" is positively defined as salvation and life transmitted through Jesus Christ. Or negatively, as salvation from sin and death transmitted through Adam.

The basic hypothesis about our human nature on which this code is built, magisterially propounded by Augustine, is that death, the primary and conclusive evidence of mutability in all species, is not a natural change of state for us. Rather, God imposed death on our species as punishment for the sin of a human individual, Adam. Consequently, this divinely introduced change in our genetic make-up could be redressed only by another divine intervention, and this was embodied in another human individual, Jesus. Potentially, his human conception had a similarly profound effect on human nature. Or, to be more precise, on certain individuals called Christians, who have had transmitted to them through the umbilical cord of apostolic succession the belief that Jesus is the Christ, the Savior – the one who is to save us from sin and death.

To do this he was born with a dual nature: a divine one inherited from his father, God, and a human one inherited from his mother. The divine nature ensures his exemption from the Adamic genetic transmission of sin and its effects and therefore affects his human nature also. Not only his, but his mother's conception has been declared immaculate to avoid his inheriting the stain of sin transmitted through human sexual intercourse. Therefore he is born of an immaculate, sexually intact virgin. The uniqueness of his birth ensures that his death is also unique, that it also occurred outside the human genetic causal loop and not because he is part of the loop and therefore subject to human mortality. Accordingly, (it is supposed) his death has broken the genetic chain of Adamic transmission (of death) by creating a distinct, independent Christian genealogy.

Those who carry this notional gene are deemed safe from death and given immortality. This triumphant outcome, spoken of as "victory over death", is one in which an individual divine death redresses the human effects of divine punishment for Adam's sin (1 Cor 15:45–56). In this way Christians are given a genealogical history independent of that transmitted by the "first" Adam. And the essential base-pairing from which it flows is that of one individual, Christ, integrated into another, Adam. He, and his sin, are one fixed point of reference; Christ and salvation is the other. Without that "fixity" inherent in our Christian genealogy, nothing fixed or secure would inhere in the salvation transmitted apostolically. Adam's "necessary sin," his *felix culpa*, is the condition of possibility for our salvation being secured by Christ. And of course this security would be jeopardized by the Darwinian loss of "fixity" in its human focal point, Adam.

### Seeing salvation, the language game of Christianity

The enduring internal coherence and imaginative power of this logic of Christian human exceptionalism were strikingly displayed in the National Gallery, London, during February-May 2000. Its aptly titled millennium exhibition, *Seeing Salvation*, was accompanied by a television series and an informative catalogue, and it generated such enormous interest as to put it at the top of the attendance list of United Kingdom exhibitions and fourth in world attendance records. Depending on one's point of view, it provided evidence for both stability and variation within the Christian genetic code.

Stability was built into the exhibition structure as it traced the history of the Christian iconography of salvation over the past two millennia, starting with the earliest and simplest symbols still familiar from church architecture and vestments. One of these, **IHS**, represents the name of Jesus in an abbreviation of the Greek version of his name, which itself derives from the Hebrew *Jehoshua*, which means "Yahweh [God] saves." The use of **IHS** as a

Latin acrostic became widespread throughout western Europe, where it was variously interpreted as *Iesus Hominum Salvator* (Jesus the Savior of Mankind), or *In Hoc Signo* [*Vinces*] (in this sign you shall conquer). This latter usage goes back to its use by Constantine as a military emblem consisting of an abbreviated form (*chi, ro*) of *xristos*, the Greek for Christ. Constantine had this engraved on his coins and on the banners of the imperial army. It was later used in its Latin form during the Crusades. This mutation into a militarist, triumphalist interpretation of the name "Savior," and of the nature of salvation as a battle against non-Christian religions and people, has a long and violent history which, alas, endures to this day.[5]

Change in Christian iconic usage is not necessarily for the better. The exhibition also included images of the Savior supposedly based on authentic originals. According to legend, one came into existence when Jesus himself, in response to a request for healing from King Abgar of Edessa, washed his face in water and wiped off the moisture on a towel. Miraculously, his likeness was printed on it. This likeness, known as the Mandylion, was brought to the king who, looking on it, was cured. Representations of this healing image of salvation and of the legend surrounding it have been popular in the Eastern Orthodox Churches throughout the centuries. However, the exhibition catalogue contains a photograph of Bulgarian soldiers in the first World War carrying a military banner with the Mandylion inscribed on it. This is an obvious example of an image's use being reversed. Once again, sad to say, a healing Savior mutates into a divine warrior bringing death to those outside a particular Christian lineage – in an attempt to legitimate violence against them.

### Can a living tradition stay fixed and mutable?

If we remain within this genealogical loop of the Adam-Jesus relationship, we can play different versions of the Christian theological language game. But does Christian genealogical history – the history of those who today believe that Jesus embodied the unconditional love of God open to all living beings – have to be "fixated" in this way? Is it not essential for a living tradition to evidence mutability *and* stability? How can we still hold, against all commonly accepted evidence, that at a fixed moment in time God created an individual, Adam, outside the evolutionary processes through which all other species were created? And further, how can we continue to revere the kind of God who, in order to punish that individual, would send death into the world for the first time – and for that matter, a death not confined to the species supposedly founded by Adam, but affecting all others as well? Common decency would seem to demand that if God sent a divine being into the world to save us from death, all would be eligible for salvation. But not so. In the strictest version of Christian logic, only one species, ours, and of that, only Christians of a particular lineage (usually a biblically transmitted one) can be saved.

Having discerned the moral flaws in this theological system, both in regard to others of our own species as well as to those of all other species, many thoughtful Christians have rejected the system in its entirety. What I myself have found increasingly unacceptable is the image of God that it presupposes and in which we are supposed to have been made. Such a claim understandably provokes the type of reaction attributed to the philosopher Ernst Bloch: "[If this is so,] I am an atheist — for God's sake!"

One way to deal with this moral lacuna is to take advantage of the biblical tradition to include all living beings within the remit of salvation. This means highlighting the image of a God who laid the foundations of the earth in geological time and brought forth living creatures to inhabit it; who has been blessed by all, everywhere and at all times; who does *not* deal with us according to our sins; and who does *not* have any favorites.[6] It means rethinking salvation, well-being, wholeness, and security in the light of what we know about our evolutionary history rather than restricting our view to a particular section of human history stretching over, at most, the past six thousand years.

### The traditional time scale of human history

As the recent celebrations of the "millennium" showed, this small fraction of time still dominates our perception of it, even though that fraction was deliberately marked out only in the sixth century CE. At that time, Pope John 1 asked a monk, Dionysius (Denis) Exiguus, to draw up a calendar which would also be a Christian chronology of human history. Following the practice of the day he dated events from the foundation of Rome (*ab urbe conditor*), fixing Christ's birth as 25 December 753 AUC. In 1650 the noted biblical scholar Archbishop James Ussher followed Denis' calendar in calculating a chronology (accepted by some to this day) in which the creation of the world had taken place at noon on 23 October 4004 BCE, and the end of the world would occur at noon on 23 October 1997 – that is, exactly 2000 years after the birth of Christ and 6000 after the creation of the world.[7]

Today, when the generally accepted geological time scale for the emergence of our planet is about 4,600 million years, some Christians still use Ussher's biblical chronology (although not his dates) as an accepted framework for human history. As was evident in the National Gallery exhibition, it has literally framed powerful and moving illustrations of the supposed entirety of human history. There may be variations on the themes, but the Christian chronological sequence (from the creation of the world and Adam to Christ's life and death and his return at the end of time) remains intact in almost every case.

The church historian Klaus Scholder points out that until about four hundred years ago the elements that comprise this ecclesiastical and theological historical picture agreed with those of the phenomenal world accepted by every European – and by extension every colonial European. Taken to be normative, the biblical narratives framed both the secular and the Christological pictures: indeed any divergences between them are for the most part negligible. Christ was seen to be as central to the history of the then known world as he was to the history of the Church – and to that of every individual within that world as to those within that church. Scripture was seen and read as a textbook of incomparable status and unique quality, one "older, more complete and more accurate than any other source." Scripture, church, and world history presented a unified picture. And a portrayal with such power and coherence, on which so much of the reality of faith and human experience depends, does not fade out of consciousness overnight.

In fact, says Scholder, in the period between 1550 and 1650 only intermittent signs indicate the tentative formulation of critical questions that heralded the slow re-structuring of historical and political consciousness. These challenges arose under the influence of realities external to the traditional Christian framework. Ever-expanding geographical perspectives beyond the limits of Western Europe fueled the popular imagination. Both figuratively and literally, Columbus, Magellan, and Tasman brought home new and undeniable realities to be pored over and analyzed by an increasingly literate laity. Indeed, remarks Scholder, one might have supposed that the wealth of new geographical reports that after 1500 increasingly flooded into Europe as a result of Dutch, Portuguese, Spanish, and English colonizing expeditions would have soon led to the abandonment of the prevailing threefold division of the world into Asia, Africa, and Europe – a conceit derived from the account in Genesis 9 and 10 of the occupation of the world by Shem, Ham and Japhet, the three sons of Noah.

However, that was by no means the case. Scholder concludes that in the history of discoveries, the tenacity of outmoded views remains one of the most astounding facts. And the comforting unity of Scripture, church, and history offered by the ancient view of the world would not be lightly set aside despite the difficulty of imposing chronological and rational order on a deluge of new information. The indicated degree of change in Christian imagination and self –perception made resistance to it all the stronger. The Bible continued (and still continues for many) to undergird the presupposition of the unity of historical understanding, in that history "as a whole" may be found in it, related to it, and divided in accordance with it. All this was and is possible only within a relatively closed sphere of western Christian culture.[8] And pertinent here is the fact that this history was taught and expounded as "salvation history."

### *Perspectives on salvation history begin to change*

One of the earliest and most notable attempts made to break out of this restricted timeline is a book whose manuscript was finished in 1641 but that was not published until 1655 (five years after Ussher's calculations). Written by a French Calvinist scholar, Isaac de La Peyrère, its title, *Prae-Adamitae* (Pre-Adamites) speaks for itself. It was printed first in Holland and appeared without details of printer or author, although this proved a vain precaution. During a stay in the Catholic Spanish Netherlands, La Peyrère was imprisoned, and released only after supposedly recanting his views. A run-away best seller, the book was translated from French into English and Dutch; its success may have been partly due to the extreme reactions it provoked. In 1656, after a storm of indignation, it was publicly burnt in Paris by the hangman.[9]

What was so shocking about it? His overall theory contains, among other considered heresies, the claim that on such internal evidence as the account of his death, Moses was not the author of the Pentateuch. The corollary to this is that its status as a text revealed by God to Moses, and therefore its truthfulness, was placed in question – as well, of course, as that of the Genesis narrative. He also alleged that other men and women were born before Adam, and it was Jewish history, not human history, that began with Adam. Perhaps most shocking of all was his proposal that everyone will be saved, whatever he or she believes and whether he or she is a pre-Adamite, an Adamite or a post-Adamite.[10]

This, as far as I know, stands as the first significant challenge to Augustinian Christian genealogical salvation history, and in the present context it is all the more remarkable in being contemporaneous with Ussher's reinforcement of that scheme's internal stability. It offers biblical proof (based on La Peyrère's own reading of certain biblical texts) as well as compelling arguments both for the existence of humans before Adam (otherwise why did God bother to mark Cain and where did Cain get his wife?) and for "why the establishment of the earth cannot be derived from that beginning usually associated with Adam." He argued for the pre-existence of humans on the basis of ancient Chaldean calculations; on the earliest documents from Egypt, Ethiopia and Scythia; and on newly discovered lands, including China, Mexico, and Tasmania, whose inhabitants "probably" did not descend from Adam. This marks a turning point in the relationship between the appeal to biblical or religious authority and what might be called the appeal to reason or science. Augustine's dismissal of the possible existence of the Antipodes and their inhabitants must needs be dismissed in turn by men who had been to Tasmania.[11]

Today the furor raised by the book may seem more astonishing than its content, but it still indicates the crucial significance of using evolutionary rather than genealogical time as a reference for theology. It emphasizes that whatever theological questions are presently raised – whether by the Jesus Seminar, by Darwinism or by earth system science – they cannot safely (in terms of security, stability and certainty) be confined within the parameters of a salvation history that begins with "Adam." Otherwise, such questions about revelation as the continuing manifestation of God to the earth's inhabitants are treated as if God's freedom to become manifest had to wait until our species emerged at a fixed point in time and in a certain place. In Christian terms it means reading the [pre-]existence of Jesus back into the evolutionary event of some 15 billion years ago, now called the supernova explosion or the Big Bang.

It is here that the analogy with the search for the gene can again help make an important point. The original hypothesis assumed stability as the gene's sole function. But the assumption was not the answer. Instead it provided the impetus for the search and a rough guide as to where scientists should go to find what they sought. They were free to search within those parameters. And the answer which eventually emerged in the form of DNA itself led them beyond those parameters to the point where we now see that DNA includes mechanisms of stability *and* mutability and functions only within a dynamic environment of cellular complexity.

How does that relate to our search for salvation? As with the physical gene, analysis of the Christian gene too has been slowly, even painfully leading us to the necessity of taking into account the effects of mechanisms of mutability. As La Peyrère's case amply illustrates, this occurs as a result of dynamic and complex changes in our cultural, geographical and social environment. The modern voyages of exploration – those we can now make into recently discovered texts and beyond familiar geographical boundaries into space itself – have called for mutations in Christian self-understanding. And even though they are for the most part institutionally rejected, they have claimed a place and now play a role in Christian theological history.

In an article entitled "The problem of religious freedom," theologian John Courtney Murray defined the present theological task as "tracing the stages of growth of a tradition as it makes its way through history." A further task, he said, is discerning the "growing end" of the tradition. This is usually indicated by a new question that is taking shape under the impact of the historical moment. On this premise, such questions and the search for answers to them would themselves become part of that "growing end." And as the search for the gene has shown, growth does not occur without change.

Murray goes on to say that in this way historical consciousness, which is the ability to discern what is of moment at a particular stage in our history, in some sense constitutes and acts as a necessary spur to the exercise of theological freedom. Therefore the evolution of human history, recorded as change in human societies through time, is constitutive of theological tradition, of its development through time.[12]

### The changing shape of theology today

Today, I believe, theological tradition is being shaped by a particular form of consciousness peculiar to our own historical moment. I call this ecological consciousness, that is, consciousness of our lives being embedded within the whole of life sustained by planetary earth systems, and of human history as part of and in dynamic equilibrium with earth history. At the global cultural level, scientific space exploration and technology today disclose the evolution of physical, chemical, and material earth systems which underpin our planetary interdependence. Political-economic transformations and trans-national media networks also play a part in changing our self-perception, a change that is part of the "growing end" of contemporary consciousness about the parameters and exercise of personal and national freedom. We are becoming conscious of ourselves as members of a global rather than a geographic, ethnic, or religious community; after all, climate change, the free market, and the globalized military-industrial complex clearly recognize none of those boundaries. There is a growing understanding that among the many factors limiting our autonomy are the viability of ecosystems, the operations of the free market model of economics, and our genetic inheritance. And through such inputs from our environments we are learning to accept that, rather than belonging to a species set apart in any meaningful way from the flow of evolutionary history, we too belong within the known range of emergent species on Earth.

Because of this changing consciousness, the need for mechanisms of stability seems greater than ever. And inevitably this affects our views on what we call "salvation", and on Jesus as savior. Many continue to seize on both

as timeless answers to the search for stability, as though our perception of
them has existed over the centuries in a static, detached tradition, impervi-
ous to changes in historical consciousness and the questions raised by its
growth. As in La Peyrère's day, many continue to take them to mean that
(some of) our species alone can be saved from sin and death. The premise
behind this theological apartheid is that Christians, or rather, their
Christianity, is confined within a change-free zone. But who – or what – can
live there?

Courtney Murray assumed that freedom is inextricably bound to growth
in the Christian tradition. That freedom necessarily includes our being free
to change or not to change our ideas about God. For me, it includes being
free to speak about salvation as God's love for and involvement with the
whole world, and then about that love and involvement being made manifest, for some of us, and in some ways, in Jesus. It assumes that we can talk
about Jesus' lifework constructively, and see it as our inherited task to affirm
in every way possible the mysterious nature of the relationship between
God, the world and ourselves. If we are not free to speak about salvation in
this way, then we have to ask ourselves whether or not we are free to love
God as the God of the whole earth community.

This raises important questions: Can we love God other than freely?
What kind of God wants to be loved any other way? If it were not free,
would it be love? If not, do we leave God free to love? To love anyone or
anything? And is not this kind of love the necessary condition for what we
call "salvation"?

As I said in the opening chapter, one of Luther's most valuable theological insights was the contrast he made between human love (*amor hominis*)
and divine love (*amor Dei*). Human love, he said, seeks a loveworthy object
– that is, one *we* decide is worthy of being loved. It is a condition of our
loving that we find someone we consider deserving of it. But divine love *creates* loveworthy beings. It attaches no conditions. It is truly gratuitous. The
grace of being loved by God makes all worthy of love.[13] And since by definition God's love is infinite, there can be no exclusions from that love,
whether of time, place, species, or creed. "Where is all, there all must be."

For me, to be loved by God unconditionally and to need no longer to
rely on human criteria for being worthy of that love, expresses the hope and
promise of salvation for all and for each of us. And not only for us, but for
every living being according to its kind. I find that unconditional love
expressed in what we know of the life and work and death of Jesus; and in
that sense, I see salvation expressed in him. That is because the context of
my life has set Jesus in the foreground as one who lived and spoke the truth

about God through his non-exclusive relationships with others. But that truth is in no way confined to his life or to those who see salvation in him.

For me, to say otherwise of God would constitute a theological lie. For if words about God are to mean anything, the all-encompassing mystery of God's love does not allow us to exclude any from that love. By definition, God is free to love the whole world and every living being in it, over eons of geological as well as genealogical time.

# 12

# The Wisdom of Gaia

In the opening chapter I referred to Nicholas of Cusa's concept of "learned ignorance" and to his use of it to expose the necessary limitations of any form of human knowledge. But the concept has a yet more positive aspect, for the adjective "learned" tells us that the ignorance that marks human knowledge is itself based on knowledge: that through knowing we become aware of what we do not know. Being aware of our ignorance, we seek to learn what needs to be known in order to correct it as far as possible. That is the path to human, as opposed to divine, wisdom.

Nicholas was concerned, as I am, with challenging a theological arrogance that would elevate one specific form of human knowledge to the level of divine knowledge. But more immediate concerns about our ignorance also need to be addressed. In particular, we need to be sufficiently knowledgeable about our place within the earth community to understand the need to practise ecological humility. For that is both the impetus to and reward for learning more about the earth and ourselves from the more-than-human world.

Today we have the opportunity to correct our ignorance about the earth by learning from what I call "the wisdom of Gaia." My choice of Gaia as a source of knowledge is due primarily to the fact that it is the name of a contemporary scientific theory that is based on rigorous in-depth study of the continuing evolution of the earth as that which provides the conditions necessary for life (including ours) to evolve and flourish. It is a project of contemporary wisdom that aims to understand life as a whole. On that basis it refuses to isolate one kind of knowledge, science, by cutting it off from the rest of life. Gaian science is a wisdom of the body politic and planetary, sacred and secular, human and more-than-human; and neither by nature nor intent does it exclude women's ways of knowing.

This brings me to my second point. Gaia is a very ancient Greek earth deity, a female personification of the planet itself rather than a projection of a gendered human attribute onto the earth. Her femaleness encourages us to bond emotionally with the planet, to love and respect the wisdom and fertility of her body while acknowledging that their scope is beyond any human person's grasp. We are involved in her life with all our faculties: physical, cognitive, imaginative, active, and compassionate. Living according to what we know of her wisdom means living as happily and peacefully as possible within the whole earth household.

### Human wisdom

Two complementary but sometimes contrasting images of human wisdom have long been accepted within western culture: wisdom as the work of the mind, and wisdom as the work of the hands. In both cases the work is assumed to have visible results, such as the scholar's text or the potter's vase. They are seen as the product if not indeed the proof of wisdom, the fruit of cognitive and practical aspects of knowledge, both of which can be discerned in the harmonious working together of hand and mind.

Wisdom may also be discerned in something quite intangible but nonetheless obvious, such as a way of living in or relating to the world by which one makes a significant contribution to the common well-being. One enduring image of this embodied wisdom is a tree whose fruit is the good life: one rooted both in the act of growing and in the knowledge of how to grow. It offers, so to speak, not only present nourishment but also the seeds of future wisdom which will, when properly tended, nourish generations yet to come.

This metaphor for wisdom is widespread throughout human culture in the many representations of the Tree of Life and the Sacred Tree. In Celtic folklore the hazel tree represents wisdom, while the nuts – sweet, concentrated energy encased in small, tough shells – are an emblem of the virtue.[1] In Judaism and in Christianity the metaphorical conjunction of tree, fruit, life and wisdom is common:

> Wisdom is a tree of life for those who hold her fast;
> Those who cling to her lead happy lives (Prov 3:18).

> Come to me, you who desire me, and take your fill of my
> fruits (Sir 24:19).

The wise ones within a community are seen as happy, secure, virtuous, and resourceful people. Their repertoire of knowledge, experience, and folk wisdom can be called on in crises and preserved in different ways for future consultation. And just as many varieties of tree grow in diverse environments, so many varieties of wisdom manifest themselves in countless individual folk and in different types of community. Such individuals are seen to "know how" to do something, as having "know-how." And the wise person is seen as one who succeeds (more often than fails) in integrating knowledge and work, being and doing, thought and action, reason and emotion. The wisdom that enables her or him to live well is embodied in life, in work, and in experience: it produces efficient, decisive, and often good-humored responses to life's unpredictability.

### The wisdom of Gaia

If one adopts the perspective of geological time rather than that of human history, the kind of language I have been using to describe the traditional sage can also be used to describe the wisdom of the Earth personified as Gaia. James Lovelock's Gaia theory describes the Earth behaving as a single living system, with the evolution of its crust and atmosphere merging with the evolution of living organisms into a single dynamic geophysiological process. This process provides and sustains conditions that allow life forms to emerge. Over time, these conditions are subject to variations that favor some forms of life over others: and if those variations persist, the latter forms dwindle, or even become extinct. This fact about the life of every organism and species, including our own, was noted by a well-known sage:

> To everything there is a season, and a time to every purpose
> under heaven:
>
> a time to be born, and a time to die;
> a time to plant, and a time to pluck up that which is planted;
> a time to kill, and a time to heal;
> a time to break down, and a time to build up. (Qoh 3:1–8)

Thus Gaia's wisdom or "know-how" can be seen as knowing how to regulate conditions favorable for life to emerge and to be built up, broken down and rebuilt in diverse forms over different time scales. It "knows how" to keep itself in homeostasis, that state of dynamic equilibrium from which different life forms emerged and grew abundant, thereby changing the environment as their evolution and the Earth's evolution merged into a single dynamic process.

This continually evolving process, which I characterize here as the wisdom of Gaia, has produced the planet's many beautiful and awe-inspiring living artifacts. We are just one such life form, tightly coupled with our environments and dependent on Gaia for the resources that sustain our lives. Countless life forms are known to us only as fossils, since they evolved, lived, reproduced, and died billions of years before our species emerged. The know-how evolving out of and embodied in the dynamic equilibrium of Gaia was the precondition for their emergence, as it was and is for our being alive.

Indeed that know-how is the absolute precondition for our being wise or foolish. As Gaia's wisdom precedes ours so does ours presuppose that of Gaia. Therefore our exercise of wisdom — whether as intellectual, bodily or practical knowledge — includes rational and religious recognition of and response to the fact that we play an integral part in processes which nourish all life. Human wisdom must therefore include conscious preservation of these processes in all their myriad aspects together with a commitment to the just and peaceful distribution of their fruits.

Properly speaking then, human wisdom has as its primary subject the integration of what we understand of the planet's life sustaining processes with our understanding of what it means to be alive. Wisdom, as the text in Proverbs reminds us, is about living happily and well. Both literally and figuratively, Earth's wisdom provides us with all we need to live in this way — for a time, as Qoheleth reminds us. We who live now are, along with all other living beings, the by-products of of the wisdom of Gaia, of "an entity that is alive at least to the extent that, like other living organisms, its chemistry and temperature are self-regulated at a state favourable for life" — including ours. And as living organisms, we too have what Lovelock calls "the emergent property" of self-regulation.[2]

Our wisdom will effectively manifest itself in our successfully integrating our self-regulation within the whole process of self-regulation that constitutes Gaia's wisdom. Our very existence ultimately depends on our ability to regulate our own lives within the constraints of that larger whole, and the more we succeed in this, the more blessed, the happier we are. "Happy the person who has found wisdom, the one who has acquired understanding" (Prov 3:13, LXX). *Makarios*, the Greek word here translated "happy," can also be rendered "blessed," "fortunate," or "wealthy." "Understanding," *phronesis* in Greek, refers to the Aristotelian notion of participatory, practical wisdom that finds the prudent course of action and implements it with regard for the good of the whole community. In this case it involves the good of the whole Earth community.[3]

In a consumerist culture that largely ignores both forms of self-regulation and certainly up to now has taken Gaian processes for granted, the self-regulated life, that is, one that accepts the need to live within certain constraints, will appear consciously counter-cultural. Limiting the growth of consumption as a rational response to the self-regulation inherent in Gaia's processing of resources is both counter-intuitive and extremely difficult in a culture whose mass media continually bombard us with images of a lifestyle characterized by over-consumption. But limiting consumption is a necessary corollary to a world view that brings Gaia's wisdom into focus and so into productive interaction with our own lives. For then what we know about the world will expand our self-knowledge and give us a new and radical perspective on how to live responsibly – that is, wisely.

To speak in religious terms, this wisdom focus is sharpened by a recognition of and reverence for the "total and diffuse sacrality [of life] that may be seen in the cosmic rhythms, in the return of vegetation and in the alternation of life and death."[4] Religious wisdom then becomes simply living in the light of what we know of the total and diffuse sacredness of Gaia's wisdom.

This kind of living may be simply expressed, but it is not easily achieved. For the cognitive systems of science, theology, and philosophy – the very disciplines that one might assume to be most attuned to Gaian wisdom – have beguiled us with a misunderstanding of wisdom that often frustrates that attunement. Central to the problem is the anthropocentricity of a mainstream theological, scientific and philosophical discussion centered on absolute claims about human reason that presume for our species a unique status that isolates it from all others. Such a self-image is essentially opposed to the practice of an ecological humility in which we see ourselves and our lives meaningfully integrated within and dependent on the whole Earth community of life and its self-regulatory constraints.

On the positive side, the increasingly visible and ruinous effects of our ignorance of the life support systems of Gaia have been a spur to increasing our knowledge about them. Scientific research is making those effects and their human causes increasingly transparent. Its findings are presented and discussed in a social and political context that assumes we want to continue to live well (and that means wisely) on the planet. Warnings about the consequences of our failure to do so are routinely aired in mainstream media. Global warming, the break-up of the polar icecaps, loss of biodiversity, marine and freshwater pollution are now seen as vital human concerns that threaten the dynamic equilibrium of the Gaian processes that make our lives possible. The global character of the threat demands of us a response that recognizes the Earth as a unitary whole in which our own lives are interdependent with all others.

These general remarks disclose my major argument here: that human wisdom, knowing how to live wisely, is in a very real sense dependent on knowing how Gaia "lives." It lives, as we do, through homeostasis, through what Lovelock calls *"that wisdom of the body* whereby a state of constancy is kept in spite of external or internal environmental change." Our own homeostasis keeps our temperature, blood salinity and acidity constant.[5] It does so, however, in constant interaction with and in spite of external and internal environmental change. That word "change" reminds us that homeostasis is a process that occurs over time – planetary, geological, biological, and human time. Therefore our homeostasis is also responsive to change and subject to unpredictability and death. It cannot be regarded as isolated, static, immortal or unchanging.

Nor can human wisdom. It cannot, as we saw in the previous chapter, be boxed up as discrete units of knowledge nor isolated from the practical realities of living. Neither does it appear all at once, fully formed, like Athene from the head of Zeus. However wise we may now consider ourselves, our wisdom has emerged from our processing of the wisdom generated and transmitted by antecedent life communities now long dead, that stretch back ultimately to the emergence of life itself. This is true biologically, culturally and spiritually, for each of these modalities of human life ultimately arose from the total and diffuse nature of Gaia's life processes, including the alternation of life and death. Regarding them as sacred is an appropriate human response.

### Images of divine wisdom

One of the religious reasons for this response is that throughout human history Gaia (the planet Earth, the world – in the present context interchangeable terms) has been seen, consciously or not, as the work of God's wisdom. Therefore the wisdom of Gaia is to be seen as a product of divine wisdom. As such, it is a sacred work, worthy of awe and reverence in its own right. We ourselves can similarly be seen as a product of Gaia's wisdom – the wise person being one especially capable of reverencing that wisdom and relating to all its products as a work of God. As Gandhi said, "The basic principle on which nonviolence rests is that what holds good in respect of oneself equally applies to the whole universe."

Wisdom writings within the Jewish and Christian traditions presuppose that the earth and its complex life systems are the work of God's wisdom, or indeed, of God *as* wisdom. To everything there is a season set by God. Every living thing knows that its life is in God's hand, as is the life and breath of all humankind (Job 12:7). The earth, as the product of God's thought and God's activity, is indissolubly bonded with, though distinct from, divine knowledge and divine work: "The earth is full of God's glory!" (Isa 6:3).

One of the important characteristics of Jewish wisdom writings is the belief that wisdom, characterized as knowledge of God's glory manifest in the earth, is acquired not through a process of revelation as usually under-stood, but through the rational application of the human mind, processing and synthesizing countless observations about the nature of the world and of human life. Biblical scholar Friedemann Golka points out that in this respect the empirical approach of this literature coincides with that of modern science.[6] It observes the world and its complexity and sees it as the work of God, the craftsman who created the world out of formless matter and ordered all things by measure, number and weight.

This image occurs not only in the Wisdom of Solomon (Wis 11:17f.), but in other Wisdom texts, notably Proverbs 8:27f., where wisdom, "like a master workman," is beside God during the work of creation. Similarly, in Job 28:25f. God gives the wind its force and metes out the waters by measure. Divine wisdom is closely identified in all these texts with the creation of order and the building up of matter into various forms according to what would now be deemed scientific laws.

A less definite form of this archetypal image of God the master builder and architect occurs in Genesis 6–9, a text written down in the post-exilic period of Judaism and increasingly accepted as belonging to Wisdom literature. These chapters narrate the story of Noah and the Flood, and the image of God the master architect again comes to the fore in the detailed instructions given to Noah by God for the building of the ark. They enable Noah (the representative man, the model husband and father) to build a refuge for all life. The specifications are quite exact. And because Noah follows them faithfully, he, his family, and every other living creature are saved.

This man made vessel built in accordance with God's plan is an archetypal reminder that salvation is bound up with securing the well-being of all life on earth. By means of the ark, every species is saved from extinction. God conceived and planned it, and Noah built it in accordance with the divine plan. In another text outside the conventional Wisdom canon (although obviously sharing its essential spirit), Solomon, the archetypal wise ruler, also embarks on an ambitious building program directly sanctioned and overseen by God. He first builds the temple – "The House of God" – and then he builds his own palace, and finally a house for his wife, Pharaoh's daughter (1 Kings 8).

The relevance of these particular narratives is that they reprise the earlier accounts in Genesis in which God's creation of the world according to a divine plan and order culminates in the creation from earth itself of man and woman. There lie our deepest roots in Earth's wisdom: God, the story proclaims, also made *us* according to plan. But in our later telling of the story, the divine specifications for our species included a unique feature, human reason, that was modeled, we presume, on divine reason. And this faculty, common to God and man (or so it has been restricted by tradition), enables us to read the divine plan back into the universe: to build not only human dwellings but human societies based on this prior divine order.

The important steps in this exposition lead from God the wise and rational architect of the world, to God employing practical wisdom to construct the human frame out of the earth's clay, and on to God instructing Noah how to build a dwelling-place for life. The circle of this self-referential system is closed when the archetypal wise man, Solomon, builds for God a visible dwelling of stone and timber. A thematic loop is also postulated – one cemented not with mortar, but with human lives. For Solomon assumes that if as he exhorts them to do, humans live according to the divine pattern of God's statutes and ordinances, the Temple will endure. Thus the existence of the Temple itself depends on people building their lives according to divine ordinance. If they turn aside from it "this house (the Temple) will become a heap of ruins" (1 Kgs 9:6–8).

In these narratives the self-regulatory character of what I call the wisdom of Gaia becomes the template for human wisdom in all its forms, including that of the life wisely lived. However, theological arrogance has deprived Gaia of her mediating role, for it assumes human ability to understand the divine plan directly. Worse, it arrogates to itself the template of divine wisdom and so presents human theological constructs as divine. But in reality, the Gaian template incorporates our lives, deeds, and aspirations into those of the whole earth household. And we must learn to see them in the context of its total and diffuse sacredness, in its cosmic rhythms, in the return of vegetation and the alternation of life and death. Because whether we accept it or are even aware of it, that is where we live.

While this latter conclusion may be self-evident to a scientist working from a Gaian perspective, the religious claim made in the Solomonic wisdom tradition goes much further. It holds that if we do not respect these patterns, then the one who established them, God, will no longer dwell on earth for us. Considering Solomon's claim that the way we live determines whether or not God's presence remains on earth calls for a delicate balance between theological assertion and ecological humility. Theologically, Solomon's hypothesis veers toward human exceptionalism in making God's presence conditional on our good behaviour. (Just as the Augustinian hypothesis makes death for all species God's punishment for our bad behaviour.) But ecologically, the claim that our survival depends on living according to the laws of divine wisdom as discerned in the natural order reminds us that we face extinction if we do not live in harmony with that order. The temples we have built will become ruins, none will be left to maintain them.

But what do temples stand for anyway? Earlier in the biblical narrative Solomon reveals his salutary doubt about what their existence means – in terms of our ignorance both of where divine presence resides and its existence within the universe. At the very moment the Temple is being consecrated, he cries, "Will God indeed dwell on earth? Heaven and highest heaven cannot contain thee – much less this building!" (1 Kgs 8:27). The doubt displays a theological modesty that refuses to make either God's dwelling on earth or the mode of God's presence there conditional on human desires or plans – or existence.

And we need to issue a similar warning, one that is also a plea for ecological humility, about the human-centered empiricism that claims Gaia's presence, the homeostasis enabling life's continuance on earth, to be dependent in any absolute sense on us. The future of human life may certainly depend on our self-regulation now, but that is not the same as saying that the future of *all* life depends on us.

The danger of theological arrogance is also implicit in any claim that takes the self-regulation of human life out of its proper context, the self-regulation of all life on earth. Theologically it presupposes that humanity is the essential, indeed the sole point of reference for God's relationship with the whole world. From there it is but a short step – one taken long ago in mainstream Christian teaching – to the belief that the world itself is here solely to support human beings and their relationship with God. The intrinsic value of the earth, "full of God's glory" long before we appeared, is discounted. Solomon remembered it, and was counted wise.

Paul later underlined Solomon's qualms about confining God within any kind of human structure when he stated categorically that "God does not dwell in houses made by human hands" (Acts 17:24). Unfortunately, this statement had little or no effect on subsequent Christian history or theology, but in effect remained nothing more than a pious interjection. On the contrary, Christianity's most enduring mark on the Earth, visible now from space, has been the erection of massive cathedrals, monasteries and churches, with God implicitly presumed as sole tenant, master architect, and craftsman. Their beauty and majesty have endured over centuries, but the Earth itself, structured with infinite wisdom over billions of years, far surpasses them in grandeur. Yet as Solomon understood, it neither contains God, nor can it presume to do so.

### Christian models of wisdom

Extant monasteries and cathedrals bear testimony to how thoroughly the laws governing mass, stress, extension, and weight were understood and employed by men who, consciously or not, perceived themselves as imitators of God in creating *cosmos*, an ordered world, out of *chaos* or shapeless mass. For them, the goal of human wisdom was the discovery and dramatization of that divine cosmic order. Its visible products were magnificent buildings and the virtuous life.

Here we encounter a particular and important confluence of Greek thought and Christian endeavor. Heraclitus defined Greek wisdom as "knowing the *thought* by which all things are steered through all things." Thought, or understanding "controls the phenomena as it constitutes the thinker." The world is an *intelligible* whole because it is ruled by thought, which can be understood by thinking beings. The same principle of intelligibility governs both the existence of the world and our knowledge of it. Heraclitus called this principle *logos*, or reason. For him, it was the wisdom that unifies all things and enables us to discern that unity and to proclaim it. Because *logos* directs all things, the universe is an intelligible whole. Moreover, its intelligibility is discerned through the exercise of our reason, which "directs" us too, and is our guide to the nature of existence, whether of the world or ourselves.[7]

This subsidiary loop in the concept of wisdom effectively isolates (and elevates) human wisdom as somehow "in control of" or ruling that of Gaia. It posits and fosters a human self-perception that regards the latter objectively, as something to be controlled and used for human purposes. It does so by assuming human wisdom to be uniquely related to divine wisdom. As we see in Heraclitus, before him in Pythagoras, and later in Plato, Augustine, Aquinas, Descartes, Spinoza and Leibniz, its defining characteristic is a carefully calculated blending of religion and reason, whose coherence rests on the assumption of an eternal timeless order revealed to the [male] intellect but not to the senses.[8] Within Christianity that cosmic order was and is considered definitively revealed through Christ the *logos* of God. Imitation of Christ was and is conceived of as operating at many different levels, all of which ideally reflect the link between divine and human reason that enables us to imitate what is perceived as divine. An important part of this mimetic process is the subjugation of the body and its senses to the strict control of reason.

This was and still is the final link in the self-referential chain that has held together Christian presuppositions – whether imperial, ecclesiastical, or monarchical – about the structure of the world, the structure of the human body, and the structure of society. It was definitively detailed late in the fifth century CE by Denys the Areopagite. He based the notion of Christian *mimesis* or imitation on a series of ecclesiastical triadic systems modelled on the supreme divine triad, the Trinity. Their interrelations are systematized as a series of mystical and ecclesiastical hierarchies, with the word "hierarchy" (sacred government or principle) denoting and shaping proper Christian structures.[9]

Denys' writings became influential again in the Middle Ages, being much valued by Aquinas and well known to Dante, who refers to him directly in the *Paradiso*. They kept the Platonic concept of the superiority of the intellect firmly entrenched within the Christian model of wisdom. Denys wrote, "Hierarchy is, as I understand it, *a sacred order and knowledge and activity* which assimilates as much as possible to likeness with God and, in response to the illuminations that are given it from God, raises itself (that is, what has been assimilated) to the imitation of Him in its own measure."[10] The "raising" in question elevates human beings above all others, and certain of them above the rest. (See Segundo's comment about the "upper" room, p. 36.)

The ambiguous use of the word and image "edification" is part of this hierachical, religious, and architectonic message glimpsed earlier in Solomon's edifices. It was employed to masterly effect in Hooker's defense of the continuity of the liturgy before and after the Reformation in the English Church. The aim of "the outward form of all religious actions," he argued, is "the edification of the church." For him, men are edified when their understanding is taught by actions that stir within them such suitable emotions as reverence, devotion, and attention. But the authentic communication of this effect requires that "edification" (internal and external) be conceived according to the order of divine hierarchy. Hooker quotes Denys' *Ecclesiastical Hierarchy*: "The sensible things which religion hath hallowed [that is, those which move the senses] are resemblances framed according to things spiritually understood."[11] God is revealed to the intellect, not to the senses. The sensible material order depends on that intellect being properly aligned with divine order and obeying it.

Commenting on Denys' systematizing of hierarchy within the church, Andrew Louth is struck by how masculine a picture this ordered arrangement paints. Indeed, the whole concept and conception of wisdom here, whether divine or human, is irredeemably that of masculine rationality. It is this, ultimately, which is raised above any other form of knowledge. Wisdom sprang from Zeus' head, not from Hera's womb. Divine order in the universe is revealed to male intellects. Men build (temples, houses, churches, selves) in response to divine plans revealed to men. Men rule over them as "head" of the church or the house and in control of the bodies that pray or live within them. All this has been justified within traditional Christianity as conforming to divine laws.[12]

Human knowledge of laws, however – whether of the *logos* that steers the universe, of electro-magnetism, or of Gaian process – is by its nature inadequate and has to be continually tested and revised. It is not enough, for practical purposes anyway, for us to deduce them by contemplation or by using intellect alone. James Lovelock's "intellectual" work on Gaia theory evolved out of his work at NASA on the possibility of there being life on Mars. This led him to ask, "What if the difference in atmospheric composition between the Earth and Mars is a consequence of the fact that the Earth alone bears life?" He started to consider the Earth as a whole system where self-regulation of climate and chemical composition are emergent properties that keep Earth's atmosphere favorable for life. Eighteen years earlier, he had invented the electron capture detector which became an important technological tool in tracking infinitesimal amounts of pollutants in the atmosphere.

The burgeoning field of scientific and other research based on Gaia theory shows that science, no less than theology or any other discipline, combines the shaping and refining of hypotheses, exploring their implications in practical ways, and then reformulating them in the light of difficulties raised by their results or by other hypotheses or theories. Since much of this work is "practical," the theories to which it gives birth cannot be dissociated from the work. Gaia science is a mixture of reasoning deductively from what appears self-evident (in Gaia, that the Earth is a single entity), and inductively from what is observed (the geological record and the chemical composition of the atmosphere). To be sure, the two approaches may be separated notionally as holism (deduction) and reductionism (induction) and then set in opposition to each other. But each implies the other and both are necessary; for, as Lovelock observes, "one of the great rewards of science is that sudden flash of understanding which comes when holism and reductionism meet."[13]

Yet the notion persists that they can be consistently separated and indeed ought to be. This, I think, is one of the reasons why some scientists have dismissed Gaia theory. They presuppose (!) that induction and reductionism alone is the hallmark of modern scientific method, indeed is the only proper starting point for reaching universal principles (which are then assumed to be self-evident). It is supposed that "bare facts" displayed under a microscope or written as equations are to be examined without the observer having any assumptions or attitudes about them or connections with them. The fact that this is humanly impossible does not prevent its being presupposed (under the name of objectivity) as the proper and sole criterion for science.

I mention this scientific absolutism here because its mirror image holds sway in mainstream Christian theology, where supposedly self-evident truths revealed to the intellect or to reason alone are considered the proper start-ing point for conceiving of or knowing God. This follows the Aristotelian postulate that "like is known by like," and that human reason and intellect sufficiently resemble divine reason to enable us to know God. The thoroughly sexist nature of this presupposition is clear when one considers that the inspired or revealed texts through which the knowledge of God is channeled are limited almost entirely to those attributed to or edited by male authors. And to relatively few of those within a narrow span of human history. These have been accepted as "middlemen" – literally hierarchical mediators between God's plans for the world and God's plans for human beings.

### Embodying wisdom

Now, however, the wisdom of Gaia is slowly gaining prominence. From space we receive more and more images of the original ark we call Earth, one built over billions of years for the emergence and sustaining of life, floating in space, wrapped in abundant water and oxygen that give it its characteristic blue and white appearance. It comes more clearly into focus with our growing understanding of the bodily wisdom inherent in keeping its water, its crust and its atmosphere in a living state of homeostasis.

What do I mean by the Earth being built, or rather building itself as the original ark? Thomas Huxley described the "wonderful metamorphoses of sea into land, and land into sea": the land being the work of countless sub-visible creatures over billions of years of geological time.[14] On top of that land lies a layer of soil whose composition, on close inspection, is discovered to be made up of countless organisms transforming dead vegetable and animal matter into humus. For millennia it has been worked over ceaselessly by earthworms and unseen life forms that take 500 years to create one inch of topsoil. Darwin devoted the last years of his life to studying "the formation of the superficial layer of earth commonly called vegetable mould," and concluded, as he says, "that worms created the earth." In fact, he affirms, worms "collaborate through their digestive work with man's attempts to manure and so fertilize his land. The worms all work together, as it were, doing an incredible job at a very slow rate and at a much greater depth than we do."[15] An alarming proportion of topsoil has been lost worldwide because industrialized agriculture, with its heavy machinery and use of pesticides, has compacted it, emptied it of living organisms and literally turned it into dust.

Darwin did not live to see this happen, but his own observations on mold, worms, and decaying vegetable matter did arouse in him a kind of awe. And he was sufficiently startled by his work to ask how man's work compares with that done through the agency of the earthworm. As "rude" imitators of the work of nature, he said, we need to shuffle the "traditional hierarchies," not necessarily to cut us down to size, but to help us see and fit our proper size.[16]

Our guiding images of the building of the world remain, however, those of its being actualized through intellectual processes, either divine or human, and consequently being made habitable for us through the work of human intelligence. Gaia theory offers a different kind of image: it sees the planet as a self-regulating, self-building material entity 'discovered' as such through the work of the poet, the scientist, the mystic, and those today who, whether they call themselves environmentalists or ecologists, housewives or farmers, are wise to the unpredictable, mysterious nature of our *EarthScape*.[17] The wisdom of Gaia is transparent to the kind of creative imagination evident in Darwin's view of the earthworm. Incorporating its vision reduces the notional distance between it and ourselves that has been imposed by centuries of religious, scientific, intellectual, and social presuppositions – and thereby fosters ecological humility.

This view depends on seeing the world as a meaningful whole. Arriving at that sense of the whole means "shuffling" the traditional hierarchies of wisdom until they, too, can be seen in proper perspective. Formerly they prioritized cognitive process (the head and its reason) over practical activity (the body and its senses). The priority given to rationality was and still is basic to much western teaching in such apparently disparate fields as our relationship with non-human species and the prohibition against suicide. Augustine's claim that "man's reason is the essence of his soul" was expanded on by Aquinas in summarizing the relation of rationality to the image of God. He declared that "of all parts of the universe, intellectual creatures hold the highest place because they approach nearest to the divine likeness."[18] Both the masculine formulation underlined by Louth and the denigration of the body are, as feminist theologians have noted, intrinsic parts of this teaching.

### Biblical and contemporary wisdom

We can, however, find a rather different image of wisdom if we integrate the human wisdom advocated in some of the biblical literature with the wisdom of Gaia. The latter's most obvious feature is its attachment to a body – that of a person or of the Earth. Wisdom does not appear in a disembodied state but characterizes the meaningful activity engaged in by a self-regulating entity involved with life in and around it. This is quite clear in biblical Wisdom writings that are often notable for their setting. Many reflect a popular or non-religious context insofar as such a distinction is relevant to these societies. Both the dispenser of wisdom and its recipient engage in all kinds of activities with all kinds of people: they rule a kingdom, build or manage a house, tend a garden, run an industrial production line, marry a wife or beget children.[19]

Another notable feature, later suppressed in Christianity, is the feminine aspect of wisdom. It is often personified as female: *hochmah, ma'at* and *sophia* are all feminine agent nouns used for a personified wisdom who integrates the cognitive and practical aspects of her knowledge.[20] With the coming of Christianity, their definitive separation both from the female and from each other was accomplished largely by subsuming wisdom in all its aspects under the person of Jesus. Because he alone has been acknowledged as "the wisdom of God," whatever hope there might be of acknowledging women's wisdom, or of attributing this faculty to Gaia or to the Earth, is still dismissed as neo-paganism.

Another lost feature is the universality of wisdom, especially in relation to knowledge of God. This, of course, is potentially available to every living being, not least through those things which God has made. The path from the wisdom of Gaia to the wisdom of God is open to everyone. Christianity, however, has restricted access to God's wisdom by claiming that Jesus is the only way to God. This restriction began very early in the Church's life, where it is recorded as being established on the authority of Jesus himself. Matthew 11:27 reports Jesus to have said, "All things have been delivered to me by my Father; and no one *knows* the Father except the Son and any one to whom the Son chooses to reveal him." (italics added)

Thus in a text definitive for church teaching on revelation, Jesus is presented in a dual role: as the one through whom God speaks, and as the one who creates the world. "In former times God spoke to us by the prophets, until in these days he has spoken to us by his Son, Jesus"; he is the one "for whom and by whom all things exist" (Heb 1:1; 2:10). This is the cosmic framework within which traditional Christianity sees itself as sole mediator of Jesus' knowledge of God and of divine order within the world.

But in the Wisdom literature, knowledge, our knowledge – whether of God, of the laws of nature, or of good and evil – is acquired not from revelation through men or one man alone, but through the rational application of human thought, and through sensible observation and practice based on it. Wherever we find that concept of human knowledge, its acquisition is not limited by time, place, person, race, sex, or class. Wisdom as female reshuffles established hierarchies, because once *man's* reason is no longer the only acceptable image of the divine, male rationality is not seen as the only acceptable tool for discerning cosmic laws and ordering their implementation within church and state.

Religious hierarchies then lose their exclusive and excluding claim to be sole mediators of knowledge of God. This means relinquishing the power to bar those "outside" their revelatory system from having any claim to an authentic knowledge of God. Instead human wisdom, as knowledge of divine wisdom, is taken to be experience-based, with the experience of being human as its common basis. It is far from coincidental that the distinction between folk-wisdom and the biblical variety vanishes in Solomon's eponymous Book of Proverbs. Nor is it coincidental that the low "revelatory" status of the wisdom writings relative to those called "The Law and the Prophets" has until recently relegated them to comparative neglect in Christian theological curricula.

This brief overview helps point the way towards a contemporary image of wisdom. First, it reinforces the link between a cosmic framework and a personal one in the practice of wisdom. The cosmic framework keeps us in our appropriate place, for it is commensurate with nothing less than God's relationship with the world throughout the whole of its evolution; and the wisdom embodied in the cosmos over this vast timescale is rightly seen as continuously related to divine, not human knowledge. Human understanding of the world then offers us some understanding of God through the wisdom of God manifest in the wisdom of Gaia. The proper response to this is awe, reverence, and a sense of the relative shortness of human history and of the limited knowledge attained by any one group within it. And since our lives are set within this frame of cosmic order and its self-regulatory processes, we need to understand them in order to regulate our lives wisely.

Second, this practical human wisdom that relates us to the world is not seen as confined to a particular race, sex, epoch, or class. It is and has been available to people throughout history, and the newly awakened awareness of and respect for the lifestyles and narratives of preliterate societies is a belated recognition of this. One such group whose knowledge was later detailed in the Jewish and Christian wisdom writings has left us a catalogue of what today would be called scientific Gaia research. Wisdom displays her knowledge of the following:

the ordering of the universe;
the operation of the elements;
the beginning and end and middle of times;
the turning of solstices and changing of seasons;
the cycles of years and the positions of stars;

the nature of living creatures and the disposition of beasts;
the forces of spirits and the reasonings of human beings;
the species of plants and the virtues of roots;
whatever is hidden and whatever is manifest.
(Wis 7:17–22, Long's translation)

The third obvious feature of a possible contemporary image of wisdom relates directly to the one first mentioned: its embodiment. The image of  human knowledge needed today is that of the whole person whose intellect, emotions, physicality, consciousness, spirituality, and imaginative power are engaged in living wisely. The biblical Wisdom texts help us here too, for they exhort us to discover the spirit of wisdom, to seek her out, and to love her beauty. They invite an active, passionate response from us to a sacred being who spans the world in power from end to end, and orders all things benignly. She is initiated into the knowledge that belongs to God, and, in an image of cooperation rather than subordination, she decides what works God will perform (Wis 8:1–5).

This is not dissimilar to the images evoked by James Lovelock's having named his scientific theory 'Gaia'. Reactions to the theory, whether by scientists or non-scientists, often reflect its having been given the name of a female earth deity.[21] Prevailing cultural, religious, scientific and Christian hierarchies correctly see this as having revolutionary implications.

For Gaia is the ancestress, the contemporary, and the daughter of biblical Wisdom, brought forth "before the beginning of the earth: when there were no depths, no springs abounding with water." She was beside God "like a master craftsman," God's "daily delight," rejoicing before God and rejoicing in God's inhabited world (Prov 8:23–31). She was and still is involved in building, rejoicing in, and maintaining the life of the whole Earth household. No task is too high or too lowly for her. She cares for the worm and for the elephant, for microcosm as for macrocosm, for the poor and for the rich. All are held safely together by her within the shelter of life's atmosphere. She rejoices in God's work and in her work of maintaining its life. The wise today are those who know their place within Gaia and how to occupy it humbly and happily.

Earthlings!
[God] has shown you what is good; what is asked of you.
Act justly; cherish compassion and loving kindness; walk
humbly with your God. (Mic 6:8)

# Afterword

Shortly after writing this book I went to Ireland where I heard a story that seems to sum up the journey recorded in these pages. It runs:

> A restaurant in a certain Irish town has a door onto the main street on which appears the notice: "This is the back door. The front door is at the back."

The distance inside between the doors is like that between earlier and later chapters here and, for that matter, between earlier and later stages in my own life. Like all cradle Catholics I was carried into a church through its "front" door to be baptized and was welcomed there by a male priest. Even so, as I grew up I became aware, albeit in a very unfocussed way, of others huddled outside round the "back door". They were a motley crew of other types of Christian and all non-Christians; each (supposedly) indelibly marked "sinner" and so presumed ineligible for entry.

Gradually, however, and especially as I realized how widely Jesus had used parables and as I learned more about their function – to bring about a reversal of expectation in the hearer – I began to question that permanently closed back door and to enquire about those excluded by it. After all, hadn't Jesus come to save sinners? To my astonishment, I then discovered that Jesus himself was to be found out there among them.

This led to another, even more startling discovery. Neither front nor back door actually exists – nor do the walls between them. I was then free to contemplate, as if for the first time, the earth hidden from view by those walls. As my attention focused on it, its beauty slowly revealed itself and I began to see it as what it is: home for the more-than-human community to

*[handwritten marginal note]* Reminds me of stepping outside the church – 1987

which I belong. Through its Gaian self-regulation, all beings within it throughout eons of time have been gifted with life according to their kind and have responded to that gift and to its Giver in a variety of ways.

Many of those gifted with human consciousness are now slowly learning — rather painfully, it must be said — how to live wisely and humbly within that community. This means, above all, acknowledging our dependence on earth and its life forms by giving thanks for its food-gifts and by sharing them and our common future as justly as possible and in peace. Those of us who wish may do so in the name of a God who invites and welcomes all without exception to the banquet of life.

Then, as Mark Primavesi suggests, we might waken to the vision of Sufi sage Hafiz:

> What is laughter?
> What is laughter?
> It is God waking up! O it is God waking up! . . .
> It is happiness applauding itself and then taking flight
> To embrace everyone and everything in this world. . .
> O what is laughter, Hafiz?
> What is this precious love and laughter budding in our hearts?
> It is the glorious sound of a soul waking up![1]

# Notes

## Chapter 1

1  Funk, Hoover and the Jesus Seminar, *The Five Gospels*, 321.
2  Shaw, *Black Girl*, 30-1
3  See Deut 10:17; Acts 10:34; Rom 2:11; Jas 2:1.
4  See Job 38–42.

## Chapter 2

1  Samaritans were considered from the cradle [i. e. always] as impure in a very high degree, and as causing impurity. This refers to the rule that Samaritan women were considered to be "as menstruants from the cradle," and their husbands as perpetually unclean for that reason... Because of this any place where a Samaritan lay was levitically unclean, and likewise any food or drink which had touched the place. Thus a traveller through Samaritan territory who accepted food or drink from them could never know if it was clean or not. By the same rule, moreover, the spittle of a Samaritan woman was unclean; and if one such woman stayed in a town, all spittle there was unclean." Jeremias, *Jerusalem in the Time of Jesus*, 356f.
2  Barrett, *The Gospel according to John*, 191.
3  Segundo, *The Historical Jesus of the Synoptics*, 131f.
4  Christ and the Samaritan Woman. Icon from last quarter fifteenth century, Kanellopoulos Museum, Athens.
5  Jeremias, *Jerusalem in the Time of Jesus* 375, n. 8.
6  Funk and the Jesus Seminar *The Five Gospels*, 512.

## Chapter 3

1  Crossan, *Jesus*, xiii.
2  Segundo, *The Historical Jesus of the Synoptics*, 39.
3  The presumption made by Pope Gregory the Great that this woman was a

prostitute and could be identified as Mary Magdalene has been comprehensively rebutted by Karen King. See King, "Back to the Future" in *the Once and Future Jesus,* 93–97.

4  A comparable scandal for many Christians today would be for the present Pope or Archbishop of Canterbury to wash the feet of a known homosexual at the altar during Holy Week services – and then have his feet washed by the homosexual.

5  Jeremias, *The Parables of Jesus,* 126f.

6  Jeremias, *The Eucharistic Words of Jesus,* 66.

7  Levin, *An Israel Haggadah,* 20.

8  Segundo, *Theology and the Church,* 84.

9  Johnston, *The Spirit-Paraclete in the Gospel of John,* 47.

10  Stewart, "Mixed Reception," 603f.

11  Jeremias, *The Eucharistic Words of Jesus,* 204.

12  Segundo, *Theology and the Church,* 59.

### Chapter 4

1  Crossan, *Finding is the First Act,* 53f.

2  Opoku, "The Church in Africa and Contemporary Sociological Challenges," 253.

3  Opoku, "The Church in Africa and Contemporary Sociological Challenges," 253.

4  Segundo, *The Humanist Christology of Paul,* 124.

5  Capra, *The Turning Point,* 285.

6  Sanders, *Paul and Palestinian Judaism,* 455. This does not legitimize the exclusion of polygamists from the Lord's supper, since fornication (a union between man and woman without responsibility for the woman or her children) cannot be compared to legal union between a man and his wives in which he accepts responsibility for the women and children's welfare.

7  Crossan, *The Dark Interval,* 125f.

8  Herbert, *The Works of George Herbert,* 255.

9  Herbert, *The Works of George Herbert,* 245.

### Chapter 5

1  Chilton Callaway, "Exegesis as banquet," 219–20.

2  Shaw, *Black Girl,* 61 (my italics).

3  English edition to be published by Brill.

4  Nida, "Canonicity and Bibles Today," 231–5.

5  Primavesi, *Sacred Gaia,* 24–7.

### Chapter 6

1  For further reading see Primavesi, *Sacred Gaia,* 121–36; Merchant, *The Death of Nature,* Sturgeon, *Ecofeminist Natures* and Plumwood, *Feminism and the Mastery of Nature.*

2  This is usually known as the Vincentian canon, formulated by Vincent of Lerins. See Bettenson, *The Documents of the Christian Church,* 821.

3  Abbott, *Documents of Vatican II*, 112f. On the implications of this for the relationship between Scripture and Tradition, see Moran, *Theology and Revelation*.
4  Barth, *The Doctrine of the Word of God*, 113. For a discussion of the formation of the Hebrew canon, see Blenkinsopp, *Prophecy and Canon*. See also Carr, "Canonization in the Context of Community," 22–64.
5  Hunter, *Growing into God*, 153.
6  Meyers, *Discovering Eve*, 12.
7  Meeks, *The First Urban Christians*, 9.
8  Louth, *Denys the Areopagite*, 10–11.
9  See Douglas, *Purity and Danger*, 41–57. See also the interesting discussion on the cultural basis of purity codes in Countryman, *Dirt, Greed and Sex*, 12. See also the distinctions he makes between the Israelite notion of the family and its subversion in the teachings of Jesus, 168f.
10  Meyers, *Discovering Eve*, 18.
11  Radford Ruether, *Women-Church*, 12.
12  See Radford Ruether, *Women-Church*, 78f. and 183f. on suggestions for baptismal ceremonies and other liturgies celebrating the life cycle of living beings. See also Oosterhuis, *Prayers, Poems and Songs*, 123f. for an imaginative baptismal liturgy.
13  See Pagels, *Adam, Eve, and the Serpent*. She brings out the implications for nature of Augustine's doctrine of the Fall of Adam in his debate with Julian of Eclanum, and goes into some of the reasons why Augustine's negative assessment was adopted as official orthodox teaching from then on.
14  See Thistlethwaite, *Sex, Race and God*, 85 for an interesting and challenging expansion of this notion in terms of differences between black and white women.
15  Peacocke, *Creation and the World of Science*, 279.
16  Zaehner, *Mysticism Sacred and Profane*, 33.

## Chapter 7
1  Article Nine in *The Book of Common Prayer*.
2  The subject of holiness and pollution covers a vast field, and the comment made here is meant to direct attention to the way in which the acceptance of classifications on such a basis acts, whether consciously or not, as legitimation for the exercise of power over sub-classes. For a wider discussion of a few of the religious and cultural issues involved, see Mary Douglas, *Purity and Danger*, 415–17. See also the discussion in Chapter 4 here, 38f.
3  Meyers, *Discovering Eve*, 80f.
4  There is no question here of trying to postulate either the priority of one text over the other or to argue for different authors or stages of editing. Whybray in *The Making of the Pentateuch* has successfully shown that the Documentary hypothesis is just that, a hypothesis. For a detailed literary analysis of the narrative, see Mieke Bal, "Sexuality, Sin and Sorrow," 317–38 f.
5  Trible, *God and the Rhetoric of Sexuality*, 79f.
6  Meyers, *Discovering Eve*, 81.
7  Brown, *The Body and Society*, 193f., 350f.
8  Brown, *The Body and Society*, 398–447.

9  See Brownmiller, *Against our Will*.

10 Summers, *Malleus Maleficarum*, pt. 2, sec. 6. See Merchant, *The Death of Nature*, 32–142; See also Starhawk, *Dreaming the Dark*, 189. The persecution of Witches was linked to three interwoven processes: the expropriation of land and natural resources; the expropriation of knowledge; and the war against the consciousness of immanence, which was embodied in women, sexuality and magic. See also Condren, *The Serpent and the Goddess*, 166f.

11 Condren, *The Serpent and the Goddess*, 173.

12 Brown, *The Body and Society*, 422, 427.

13 Condren, *The Serpent and the Goddess*, 173.

## Chapter 8

1  See Wiles, *The Christian Fathers*, 18.

2  Meyers, *Discovering Eve*, 77, 87.

3  Quell, *Sin*, 15. The story of the "fall", Quell says, affords a panoramic view of human life. He does not agree with the suggestion of another scholar that the creation of woman may have been the result of sin, i.e. an act of divine anger [sic], and rebukes yet another scholar for saying that this is fairly certain. This footnote skirmish is a useful example of the general tenor of male scholarly interpretation of Genesis, especially when Quell states that the aetiological interpretation of the myth of the Fall "undoubtedly justifies our basing upon it a theory of "original sin" in the sense of man's universal sinfulness."

4  Quell, *Sin*, 23. Compare this with Meyers, *Discovering Eve*, 87f.

5  Gen 3:23. Korsak translates the Hebrew: "YHWH Elohim sent it [the groundling] from the garden of Eden to serve the ground from which it was taken." (Korsak 1993:11) See also Meyers, *Discovering Eve*, 50f.

6  The effects of this assumption on the Christian doctrine of resurrection are powerfully argued in Pohier, *God – in Fragments*. I look in some detail at the role of death in life, and at our attitudes towards it, in *Sacred Gaia*, and even more thoroughly in *Gaia's Gift*.

7  See Pagels, *Adam, Eve and the Serpent*, 130–50, for a full and fascinating discussion of the issues raised in their debate and summarized here. See also *Gaia's Gift*, 91–8.

8  Trible, *God and the Rhetoric of Sexuality*, 139.

9  Pagels, *Adam, Eve and the Serpent*, xix. See also Hillman, *The Myth of Analysis*, 218 and Radford Reuther, *Womanguides*, 81–102.

10 Wiles, *The Christian Fathers*, 29.

## Chapter 9

1  See Brenner, *The Israelite Woman*, 122–31, and Segundo, *The Humanist Christology of Paul*, 176.

2  For a related discussion of structural sin, see Segundo *The Humanist Christology of Paul*, 174f. See also Mollenkott, *Godding*, 41. For a detailed discussion of it within the context of an ecological paradigm, see *Sacred Gaia*, 164–7.

3  Judith Plaskow in a lecture at the European Society of Women in Theological Research, Arnoldshein, 1989, pp. 16f. See also Virginia Mollenkott's ques-

tioning along the same lines of the God revealed in the Job narrative in *Godding*, 29. This type of questioning is what I understand Pohier to mean by "the decomposition of God."

4 Segundo, *An Evolutionary Approach to Jesus of Nazareth*, 84f.

5 Meyers, *Discovering Eve*, 82–5.

6 Meyers, *Discovering Eve*, 82–5. See also Landy, *Paradoxes of Paradise*, 226. On the Genesis narrative, he says that the repetition and variation amplify the statement with purely emotive effect. The duplication of language suggests a surcharge of meaning contained within the metrical structure.

7 Meyers, *Discovering Eve*, 50–63.

## Chapter 10

1 Leighton, *The Philosophy of Gardening*.

2 Hardy, *Selected Poems*, 94.

3 See Lovelock *Gaia*, 133–152.

4 See Primavesi, "Ecology". See also first four chapters in *Gaia's Gift*.

5 A free rendering of the passage in Bertolt Brecht, *Life of Galileo*, 53f. I examine this and other pertinent aspects of the Copernican revolution in detail in *Gaia's Gift*.

6 See, for example, Margulis and Sagan, *What is Life*. Also Lamb and Sington, *Earth Story*, with accompanying TV series.

7 Rozenzweig, *The Star of Redemption*, 112f.

8 Hardy, *Selected Poems*, 94.

## Chapter 11

1 Fox Keller, *The Century of the Gene*, 12.

2 Fox Keller, *The Century of the Gene*, 13f.

3 Fox Keller, *The Century of the Gene*, 23f.

4 Fox Keller, *The Century of the Gene*, 31–43.

5 See Primavesi, *Sacred Gaia*, 145–47.

6 Job 38–42; Pss 102, 103; Deut 10:17; Acts 10:34; Rom 2:11; Jas 2:1

7 Gould, *Time-scales and the Year 2000*, 8–13.

8 Scholder, *The Birth of Modern Critical Theology*, 67–79.

9 Scholder, *The Birth of Modern Critical Theology*, 82–87.

10 Popkin, *Spinoza and La Peyrère*, 183.

11 Popkin, *Spinosa and La Peyrère*, 184–5; Scholder, *The Birth of Modern Critical Theology*, 86–89.

12 Courtney Murray, "The Problem of Religious Freedom," 569.

13 Luther, *Heidelberg Disputation*, 1518, Conclusion 28.

## Chapter 12

1 Craighead, *The Sign of the Tree*, 148.

2 Lovelock, *Gaia: The Practical Science of Planetary Medicine*, 11, 187.

3 Primavesi, "The Recovery of Wisdom," 83.

4 Ricoeur, *Figuring the Sacred*, 52.

5 Lovelock, *Gaia: The Practical Science of Planetary Medicine*, 188 (my italics).

6  Golka, *The Leopard's Spots*, 114f.
7  Frankfort, *Before Philosophy*, 255f.
8  Russell, *History of Western Philosophy*, 56.
9  Louth, *The Origins of the Christian Mystical Tradition*, 159.
10 Louth, *The Origins of the Christian Mystical Tradition*, 169 (my italics).
11 Louth, *Discerning the Mystery*, 90f.
12 Primavesi, *Sacred Gaia*, 121–136.
13 Lovelock, *Gaia: The Practical Science of Planetary Medicine*, 35f.
14 Huxley, "On a Piece of Chalk," 17.
15 Phillips, *Darwin's Worms*, 45.
16 Phillips, *Darwin's Worms*, 50.
17 Primavesi, *Sacred Gaia*, 85–88.
18 Rachels, *Created from Animals*, 89.
19 Harrington, *The Wisdom Texts from Qumran*, 41,
20 Long, *In a Chariot Drawn by Lions*, 80–118.
21 Primavesi, "The Recovery of Wisdom," 78f.

### Afterword

1 Ladinsky, *I heard God Laughing*, 125.

# Works Consulted

Abbott, W., Ed. *The Documents of Vatican II.* Piscataway, New York: America Press, 1966.

Abram, D. *The Spell of the Sensuous: Perception and Language in a More-Than-Human World.* New York: Pantheon Books, 1996.

Bal, M., Ed. *Anti-Covenant: Counter-Reading Women's Lives in the Hebrew Bible.* Sheffield: Almond Press, 1989.

Barrett, C. K. *The Gospel according to John.* London: SPCK, 1955.

Barth, K. *The Doctrine of the Word of God.* Edinburgh: T and T Clark, 1936.

Bettenson, H., Ed. *Documents of the Christian Church.* Oxford: Oxford University Press, 1963.

Brecht, B. *Life of Galileo.* London: Methuen, 1980.

Brenner, A. *The Israelite Woman.* Sheffield: JSOT Press, 1985.

Brown, P. *The Body and Society.* New York: Columbia University Press, 1990.

Brownmiller, S. *Against our Will: Men, Women and Rape.* London: Secker & Warburg, 1975.

Capra, F. *The Turning Point.* London: Fontana, 1983

Carr, D. "Canonization in the Context of Community." Pp. 22–64 in *A Gift of God in due Season: Essays on Scripture and Community in Honor of James A. Sanders.* Eds. Richard D. Weis and David M. Carr. Sheffield: Sheffield Academic Press, 1996

Chilton Callaway, M. "Exegesis as Banquet: Reading Jeremiah with the Rabbis." Pp. 219–31 in *A Gift of God in due Season: Essays on Scripture and Community in Honor of James A. Sanders.* Eds. Richard D. Weis and David M. Carr. Sheffield: Sheffield Academic Press, 1996

Christ, C., and Plaskow J., Eds. *Womanspirit Rising: A Feminist Reader in Religion.* San Francisco: Harper & Row, 1979.

Comblin, J. *The Holy Spirit and Liberation.* Maryknoll, New York: Orbis Books, 1989.

Condren, M. *The Serpent and the Goddess.* San Francisco: Harper & Row, 1989.

Countryman, L. *Dirt, Greed and Sex: Sexual Ethics in the New Testament and Their Implications for Today*. London: SCM Press, 1989.

Courtney Murray, J. "The Problem of Religious Freedom" in *Theological Studies*, 25 (1964) 506ff.

Craighead, M. *The Sign of the Tree*. London: Mitchell Beazley, 1979

Crossan, J. D. *The Dark Interval*. Illinois: Argus Communications, 1975.

––– *Finding is the First Act*. Philadelphia: Fortress Press, 1979.

––– *Jesus: A Revolutionary Biography*. New York: Harper Collins, 1994.

Douglas, M. *Purity and Danger*. London and New York: Ark Paperbacks, 1989.

Dunn, J. *Jesus and the Spirit*. London: SCM Press, 1975.

Fox Keller, E. *The Century of the Gene*. Cambridge Mass: Harvard University Press, 2000.

Frankfort, H., Wilson, J. A, Jacobsen, T. *Before Philosophy*. London: Penguin, 1949.

Funk, R. W., Hoover R. W. and the Jesus Seminar. *The Five Gospels*. New York: Polebridge Press, 1993.

Golka, F. W. *The Leopard's Spots: Biblical and African Wisdom in Proverbs*. Edinburgh: T&T Clark, 1993.

Gould, S. J. *Time Scales and the Year 2000*. London: Penguin, 2000.

Hardy, T, *Selected Poems*. London: Penguin, 1978.

Harrington, D. *Wisdom Texts from Qumran*. London and New York: Routledge, 1996.

Herbert G. *The Works of George Herbert in Prose and Verse*. London and New York: Warne and Co., (undated).

Hillman, J. *The Myth of Analysis*. New York: Harper Torch Books, 1978.

Hunter A. "Gone Fishing or Saussure or not so sure." Pp. 145–55 in *Growing into God* London: CTBI Press, 2003.

Huxley, T. *Lectures and Lay Sermons*. London: Dent and Son, 1910.

Jeremias, J. *The Parables of Jesus*. London: SCM Press, 1963.

––– *The Eucharistic Words of Jesus*. London: SCM Press, 1966.

––– *Jerusalem in the Time of Jesus*. London: SCM Press, 1969.

Johnston, G. *The Spirit-Paraclete in the Gospel of John*. Cambridge: Cambridge University Press, 1970.

King K. "Back to the Future." Pp. 77–107 in *the Once and Future Jesus*. Santa Rosa: Polebridge Press, 2000.

Korsak, M. P. *At the Start: Genesis Made New*. New York: Doubleday, 1993.

Landinsky, D. *I Heard God Laughing: Renderings of Hafiz*. California: Danial Ladinsky Books, 1996.

Landy, F. *Paradoxes of Paradise: Identity and Difference in the Song of Songs*. Sheffield: The Almond Press, 1983.

Leighton, C. *The Philosophy of Gardening*. Newbury: Croft Publications, 1991.

Levin, M. *An Israel Haggadah*. New York: Abrams Inc., (undated).

Liebes, S., Sahtouris, E. and Swimme, B. *A Walk Through Time: From Stardust to Us*. New York: Wiley, 1998.

Long, A. *In a Chariot Drawn by Lions*. London: The Women's Press, 1992.

Louth, A. *Denys the Areopagite*. Wilton, Conn.: Morehouse-Barlow, 1989.

――― *Discerning the* Mystery. Oxford: Clarendon Press, 1983.

――― *The Origins of the Christian Mystical Tradition.* Oxford: Clarendon Press, 1981.

Lovelock, J. *Gaia, The Practical Science of Planetary Medicine.* London: Gaia Books, 1991.

Luther, M. Heidelberg Disputation, 1518, Conclusion 28. Weimar:1883.

Margulis, L. and Sagan, D. *What is Life?* London: Weidenfeld and Nicholson, 1995.

McDaniel, J. *Earth, Sky, Gods and Mortals.* Mystic, Conn.: Twenty Third Publications, 1989.

Meeks, W. *The First Urban Christians: The Social World of the Apostle Paul.* Newhaven and London: Yale University Press, 1983.

Merchant, C. *The Death of Nature: Women, Ecology and the Scientific Revolution.* New York: Harper & Row, Perennial Library, 1982.

Meyers, C. *Discovering Eve: Ancient Israelite Women in Context.* Oxford: Oxford University Press, 1988.

Mollenkott, V. Godding: Human Responsibility and the Bible. New York: Crossroad, 1987.

Moran, G. *Theology of Revelation.* London: Burns & Oates, 1967.

Morton, N. *The Journey is Home.* Boston: Beacon Press, 1985.

Naess, A. "Modesty and the Conquest of Mountains." Pp. 13–17 in *The Mountain Spirit.* Eds. Tobias, M. C. and Drasdo, H. London: Victor Gollancz, 1980.

Nida, E. A. "Canonicity and Bibles Today." Pp. 231–36 in *A Gift of God in due Season: Essays on Scripture and Community in Honor of James A. Sanders.* Eds. Weis, R. D. and Carr, D. M. Sheffield: Sheffield Academic Press, 1996.

Opoku, K. A. "The Church in Africa and Contemporary Sociological Challenges", Pp. 241–255 in *The Ecumenical Review,* Vol. 40, No. 2. 1988.

Pagels, E. *Adam, Eve, and the Serpent.* London: Penguin Books, 1990.

Peacocke, A. *Creation and the World of Science.* Oxford: Clarendon Press, 1979.

Phillips, A. *Darwin's Worms.* London: Faber and Faber, 1999.

Plumwood, V. *Feminism and the Mastery of Nature.* London: Routlegde, 1993.

Pohier, J. *God in Fragments.* London: SCM Press, 1987.

Popkin, R. H. "Spinoza and La Peyrère." Pp 182–92 in *Southwestern Journal of Philosophy* 8. 1977

Primavesi, A., and Henderson, J. *Our God Has No Favourites.* San Jose, Ca.: Resource Publications, 1989.

――― *From Apocalypse to Genesis: Ecology, Feminism and Christianity.* Tunbridge Wells and Minneapolis: Burns & Oates and Fortress Press, 1991.

――― "The Recovery of Wisdom." Pp 73–86 in *Spirit of the Environment.* Eds. Cooper, D. E. and Palmer, J. A. London: Routledge, 1998.

――― "Ecology." Pp. 187–89 in *The Oxford Companion to Christian Thought.* Ed. Hastings, A. Oxford and New York: Oxford University Press, 2000a.

――― *Sacred Gaia: Holistic Theology and Earth System Science.* London and New York: Routledge, 2000b.

――― *Gaia's Gift: Earth, Ourselves and God after Copernicus.* London and New York: Routledge, 2003.

Quell, G. et al. *Sin, Bible Key Words.* London: A & C Black, 1951.

Rachels, J. *Created from Animals: The Moral Implications of Darwinism.* Oxford and New York: Oxford University Press, 1990.

Radford Ruether, R. *Sexism and God-Talk: Towards a Feminist Theology.* Boston: Beacon Press, 1983.

––– *Womanguides: Readings Towards a Feminist Theology.* Boston: Beacon Press, 1985.

––– *Women-Church: Theology and Practice.* San Francisco: Harper & Row, 1988.

Ricoeur, P. *Figuring the Sacred.* Minneapolis: Fortress Press, 1995.

Rozenzweig, F. *The Star of Redemption.* Trans. W. W. Hallo, Indiana: Notre Dame Press, 1985.

Russell, B. *History of Western Philosophy.* London: Allen and Unwin, 1975.

Sanders, E. P. *Paul and Palestinian Judaism.* London: SCM Press, 1977.

Scholder, K. *The Birth of Modern Critical Theology.* London: SCM Press, 1990.

Segundo, J. L. *An Evolutionary Approach to Jesus of Nazareth.* Maryknoll, New York: Orbis Books, 1988.

––– *Faith and Ideologies.* Maryknoll, New York: Orbis Books, 1984.

––– *The Historical Jesus of the Synoptics.* Maryknoll, New York: Orbis Books, 1985.

––– *Theology and the Church.* London: Geoffrey Chapman, 1985.

––– *The Humanist Christology of Paul.* Maryknoll, New York: Orbis Books, 1986.

Shaw, G. B. *The Adventures of the Black Girl in Her Search for God.* London: Constable and Co., 1932.

Starhawk. *Dreaming the Dark.* London: Mandala, Unwin Paperbacks, 1982.

Sturgeon, N. *Ecofeminist Natures.* New York: Routledge, 1997.

Thistlethwaite, S. *Sex, Race and God: Christian Feminism in Black and White.* London: Geoffrey Chapman, 1990.

Trible, P. *God and the Rhetoric of Sexuality.* Philadelphia: Fortress Press, 1978.

Whybray, R. *The Making of the Pentateuch.* Sheffield:JSOT Press, 1987.

Wiles, M. *The Christian Fathers.* London:SCM Press, 1977.

Zaehner, R. *Mysticism Sacred and Profane.* Oxford: Oxford University Press, 1957.

# Index of Citations

# Index